The Corporate Angel Network
http://www.corpangelnetwork.org/
Westchester County Airport, One Loop Road
White Plains, NY 10604
(914) 328-1313

Nonprofit organization provides free plane transportation for cancer patients using empty seats aboard corporate aircraft operating on business flights.

National Patient Air Transport Helpline
http://www/npath.org
(800) 296-1217; outside the U.S.: (757) 318-9145

Service of the National Charitable Patient Air Transportation System; provides free information and referrals to patients needing free or discounted air travel.

The Andy Bovin Memorial Fund
C/O The Overlook Foundation Hospital
36 Upper Overlook Road
P.O. Box 220
Summit, NJ 07902-0220

This fund, established in memory of Andy Bovin, who died after his battle with leukemia at age six, provides support and funding for expenses that aren't covered by insurance for families of children with pediatric cancers. The funds can be used for things like travel to see a sick child, or even a trip to Disneyland for the family before a child enters treatment. Also funded is the Family Education Manual for the Valerie Fund Children's Center, a highly useful resource for families navigating their way through a child's cancer treatment.

SURVIVOR

TAKING CONTROL OF
YOUR FIGHT
AGAINST CANCER

LAURA LANDRO

SIMON & SCHUSTER

SIMON & SCHUSTER
Rockefeller Center
1230 Avenue of the Americas
New York, NY 10020

SIMON & SCHUSTER and colophon are
registered trademarks of Simon & Schuster Inc.

Designed by Ruth Lee

Manufactured in the United States of America

1   3   5   7   9   10   8   6   4   2

Library of Congress Cataloging-in-Publication Data

Landro, Laura, date.
Survivor : taking control of your fight against cancer / Laura Landro.
p.   cm.
1. Landro, Laura, date—Health.   2. Leukemia—Patients—
New York (State)—New York—Biography.   3. Women journalists—
New York (State)—New York—Biography.   I. Title.
RC643.L43   1998
362.1'9699419'0092—dc21   98-27002   CIP
[B]

ISBN 0-684-84335-8

ACKNOWLEDGMENTS

As a journalist who mostly writes about other people, I might never have written about my own struggle with leukemia without the encouragement of my colleagues at *The Wall Street Journal*—Larry Rout, Dennis Kneale, John Blanton, Dan Hertzberg, and Paul Steiger—who initially asked me to use my own story to illustrate for our readers the importance of taking control of your own destiny in a health crisis. I also want to thank Ed Bleier and my agent, Mort Janklow, who both encouraged me to think about expanding that story into a book. I owe my greatest thanks to my editor, Michael Korda, whose own frank account of his battle with prostate cancer, *Man to Man,* served as a true inspiration.

This book would not have been possible without the help of my mother, Beverly Landro, whose meticulous diary helped me piece together events that took place when I was hospitalized and barely conscious of them. I am also indebted to other cancer survivors who shared their stories with me and particularly to Susan Stewart of the *Blood and Marrow Transplant Newsletter* and Laurel Simmons, founder of BMT-Talk, whose pioneering work has made cyberspace a friendly destination for the afflicted.

The others I need to acknowledge are all characters in this book, and I hope in describing their roles in saving my life I can begin to convey my eternal gratitude. I also owe special thanks to Tom Brokaw for his eloquence, support, and rice pudding; to Denis Bovin for his courage and friendship; and to Tom King for always being there to cheer me up during the darkest times with the Hollywood Minute. Finally, thanks to all my friends in the Marine Corps. I feel like I'm almost one of you now. Semper Fi.

For my parents, who gave me life,
For my brothers, who saved my life,
And for Rick, who made it worth living

CONTENTS

INTRODUCTION

The day you learn you have cancer or any life-threatening illness, you cross over into a parallel universe, a world that separates you from everyone else except those who have been through the same thing. If you are one of the unlucky ones, it will hit when you least expect it, probably at the prime of your life, when you are at the top of your game, reaching the pinnacle of your career. It won't care. No amount of money or success can stop it. The fact that you've just had a child, or fallen in love, or gotten a big promotion, or landed a new client won't matter, either.

There may have been something you could have done to prevent it, like stopping smoking or finding a job that didn't expose you to toxic substances. But more likely than not, the disease was mapped into your genes from birth or triggered by something you couldn't have avoided. There's no use trying to figure out why you, why now. Questions are irrelevant, because it won't wait for answers.

I learned all this seven years ago, when it happened to me, when I learned I had leukemia. There are no precise statistics on how many others go through the same thing each year and new cancer cases declined for the first time in 1997. But the American Cancer Society recently estimated that there will be 1.23 million new cases of cancer diagnosed in 1998 alone. Though the chances of developing some form of cancer increase with age, it is the young and middle-aged who have the most to lose. According to recent research done by the cancer group, one out of every sixty men and one of every fifty-two women developed an invasive cancer by the age of thirty-nine. But between the ages of forty and fifty-nine, a time many view as the prime of life, that number leapt to one in every twelve men and one in every eleven women. Fortunately, overall cancer deaths are declining; you want to do what you can to be on the decline curve of those statistics.

I was trained as a journalist, so digging up facts and statistics and reporting on my disease and its treatment came easily to me. But you don't have to be an investigative reporter in order to learn all you can about something that threatens to destroy you, and then intelligently analyze your options for treatment. Even the august *New York Times* recently declared that this is the age of the self-educated patient. For while science has made huge strides in early detection and treatment of cancer, and in the end, of course, you must rely on medical experts to treat your disease, it does not mean you must or should simply abrogate your responsibility and leave the decisions to doctors and hospitals.

A woman who once called me for advice after being diagnosed with cancer asked me in frightened tones, "But how could you tell the doctors you didn't trust their opinions? What if they got mad at you and didn't want to help you?" She seemed amazed at the idea that you could simply fire a doctor who wasn't giving you the answers you needed or the attention and care you deserved. But you can do exactly that.

Americans are great consumers—we know how to get information on the best new car, the best mutual fund, the best college for our kids. Think of health care the same way, and you won't be as daunted. The key to survival is taking control, learning everything you can about your treatment, making informed decisions, and being prepared to fight if necessary: for the right care, the right doctors, and in the end, for your own life. Had I not done this, I might not be alive today.

As unlucky as I was to have cancer at a young age, I know I was fortunate in almost every other way. I had a loving, supremely functional family and devoted friends, all of whom threw themselves into the task of helping to research my care and save my life. I had connections, financial resources, and insurance. I realize there are many people who have none of these advantages, and for whom my story might seem to have less relevance. But, in fact, there are in this country resources, information, and help available for those less fortunate. Financial or any other status has no real significance when it comes to fighting disease. Everyone has the right—and the obligation—to participate actively in the crucial medical decisions whose outcome will determine his or her survival.

And it is important to remember that one is never alone in the fight. There are thousands of others who have gone through the same thing, and whose experience can help guide you. You probably already have friends, loved ones, and family members who are ready to line up by your side to help you navigate your way through this frightening new world. In addition to science and analyses, love and loyalty mean a great deal when you are fighting for your life. Your relationships will be sorely tested, but the ones that are worth having will survive with flying colors.

Sometimes cancer strikes in such an advanced stage or in a form so acute that there may be little time for intensive research, or the patient may be too sick to do it. That's when an advocate is needed: a spouse or parent or friend who can do the research, quiz the doctors, and weigh the alternatives. That may be the role you've assumed, and it is someone you love who is going through this terrible process. I've known many brave mothers, fathers, husbands, and wives who have shouldered the responsibility of educating themselves. Someone has to do it.

The technology revolution and the Internet have put a world of information at your fingertips; using your home or office computer, or relying on a friend or family member who has one, or even utilizing one at the local library, you can instantly get access to a vast array of clinical information, including case studies, survival rates, and up-to-date facts about any disease. There are patient-advocate organizations springing up all over the country that can help you sort through the reams of data you will encounter, and guide you in negotiating your way around the medical system.

It's important to understand that this isn't just a strategy for people who can afford the luxury of several opinions or who have a flexible health care plan—taking control is equally possible for people in even the most restrictive managed care plans. In fact, with the era of managed care you need to be more informed than ever, since many HMOs try to force you to use providers approved by them that may not necessarily be the best ones. There is already a huge backlash in this country against such practices. If you educate yourself about your care, you have a much better chance of fighting the system. States are already passing bills to protect patients from HMOs who put profit over proper care. And yes, there are many wonderful and caring doctors and others in the medical community who will support your quest for the best possible care and the most advanced therapies available.

When I was faced with cancer, I found plenty of books by psychologists and doctors on how to cope psychologically and philosophically. I found others by celebrities who told heartwarming stories of beating the odds. There were books on natural healing and miracles. They were all well and good, but what I wanted to know was how to go about actively trying to save my own life, and what I learned is what I have tried to set out here. It wasn't my intention to write a medical treatise or to dwell on the gory details of my ordeal, but it was necessary to do a little of both to explain what happens when you have to go through something such as this. I hope to offer my experience as a guide to people negotiating their way through this perilous new world. It's your life, and it's up to you to save it.

SURVIVOR

THE BAD NEWS

On the afternoon of August 20, 1991—my thirty-seventh birthday—I was in my apartment in New York City, trying to muster some energy to celebrate. For weeks, I had been feeling increasingly tired and out of sorts. My parents were in town to take me out to dinner at my favorite Italian restaurant, and the following day we were planning to drive to Long Island for a family vacation at the beach, a period of rest that I hoped would do me some good. Too bad I'm not there already, I thought. I suddenly had such a crushing sense of fatigue that I decided to lie down for a few minutes.

Three hours later, it took all the strength I had just to get up off the bed again. Something has got to be wrong with me, I thought to myself as I stared at my pale face in the mirror, trying with makeup to cover the dark circles under my eyes.

But what was it that was wrong? Had I been staying out too late, not taking good enough care of myself, working too hard? My job—managing a dozen reporters and writing about the entertainment industry for *The Wall Street Journal*—entailed more than its share of stress, but not enough to make me feel *this* tired. If anything, life at the newspaper was energizing; I did my best work on the adrenaline of deadlines. I had always been in good health. And though I was no athlete, after years of regular exercise, I had never been in better physical condition.

Like most people, I had my share of modern day health paranoia, illogically wondering if a bad headache could be a brain tumor. Each of my father's four sisters had battled breast cancer. That put me in a higher risk category, and I worried about it. But when you came right down to it, I regarded illness and disease as the curse of the old and infirm, a vague concern for the distant future. I decided whatever was ailing me now must be some temporary aberration, a virus, something I would soon shake off.

The next day we arrived in Southampton to stay at a friend's oceanfront house. I looked forward to being outside every day—riding my bike, running, swimming laps in the heated pool. But when I tried to exercise, the effort left me winded, gasping for breath. I complained to my mother that I had never felt so run down. As a nurse, she had always been a better diagnostician than the average mother, and she, too, was worried. "You look so pale and tired," she told me as we walked along the beach one morning. "Why don't you see a doctor as soon as you get back home?"

I promised her I would, but after I returned to work in September, things got so hectic that I put off making an appointment. I figured if I ignored it, maybe it would go away. But it didn't. In fact, some mornings, I felt as if I were nailed to my bed, unable to shake off sleep without great effort. There was a nagging ache in my left side that sometimes intensified into a sharp pain. A surge of that adrenaline would get me through the pressure-cooker afternoon deadlines at the office, but I was so spent at night that I would often have to lie down in the back seat of a taxi on the way home.

As if I needed a further incentive to see a doctor, a notice arrived in the mail from Dow Jones, the parent company of *The Wall Street Journal,* offering to pay for a complete annual physical as part of a new health plan. Finally I stopped procrastinating. On the morning of Tuesday, October 22, I went to see Dr. Steven Marks, who had treated me for the occasional flu or stomach virus, and I told him about my symptoms. "You look fine," he said after examining me in his office. "But let's do some blood work just to be sure."

Two days later, on Thursday, October 24, I was in my office, thinking of little else but a story I was writing for the next day's paper. The newsroom was in its usual state of contained pandemonium, reporters hammering away at their computer terminals, the fax machine spewing out press releases, the phones ringing incessantly. I was still waiting for some sources to call me back with information I needed for my story. On days like this, anyone who called me on unrelated business, including my mother, was usually dispatched with a brusque, "Can't talk now, I'm on deadline."

I picked up the phone at about 3 P.M., blanking on the name for a second when the caller said, "Laura, Steven Marks here." Realizing who it was, I assumed it was a courtesy call from the nice doctor to tell me my malaise was all in my head; I had actually been feeling a little better that day. "What's up, Doc?" I chirped, still mostly focused on the computer screen in front of me. But his tone as he answered was grave. What he was about to tell me would divide my life into everything before this phone call, and everything after.

"Well, your blood tests have come back, and there's a problem," Dr. Marks began. "Your white blood cell count is extremely elevated."

He suddenly had my undivided attention. "Like, how elevated?" I asked, feeling a prick of alarm. Dr. Marks replied that my white blood cell count was close to 75,000, while the normal level was closer to 4,000. My alarm intensified. "But what does that mean?" I asked.

"It could be an infection, but there's nothing else in the blood test that indicates that," Dr. Marks said. With my reporter's instincts kicking in, I pressed him harder. "Dr. Marks, what else could this be? What is the worst case scenario here?" I asked.

"Well," he said carefully, "I've consulted a hematologist, and he says it looks like something called chronic myelogenous leukemia."

I heard the word "leukemia" and a wave of panic washed over me. I felt disoriented, and my heart started to pump faster in my chest. I wasn't even sure exactly what leukemia was, but I knew it had to do with the blood, and that it was a form of cancer. A friend's son had died of it a decade earlier after a desperate battle that took up most of his short life. "Leukemia," I repeated, then asked incredulously, "are you telling me I'm going to die here?"

"Of course not," Dr. Marks said, assuring me I was in no immediate danger. "But a hematologist I work with can see you today if you want. Why don't you get there this afternoon?" I jotted down the name and address he gave me, and told him I would head there straight away.

As I hung up the phone in a daze, I glanced up to see my friend and colleague Alix Freedman, one of the paper's best reporters and an equally good eavesdropper, in my doorway. She had been standing there long enough to hear most of my end of the conversation. "What is going on?" she whispered. I shakily relayed what Dr. Marks had said, and told her I had to leave the office right away. "I'm coming with you," she said, and ran off to call a car service for us.

Mechanically, I made the calls necessary to enable me to walk out of the office in the middle of a really important story, which suddenly didn't seem so important anymore. I called Marty Schenker, the national news editor, and told him a medical emergency had come up; he would have to find something else to fill the big space where my story was supposed to go. Something in my voice told him not to argue with me. My deputy, Dennis Kneale, agreed without question to edit any other stories that broke that afternoon. Finally, I called the executive who was the main subject of my story and told him it was on hold for today.

I gathered my briefcase, coat, and purse, and walked out with Alix to the waiting car. We headed up the FDR Drive, the quickest route to the upper East Side from lower Manhattan. Mercifully, for once there was no traffic. I stared out at the sun glinting off the familiar city skyline, the tugboats pushing barges down the East River, the graceful bridges linking Manhattan to Brooklyn and Queens. It was a perfect day, but to me everything seemed unreal. I couldn't stop tears from welling up in my eyes. "I can't believe this, I just can't believe this," I kept saying. Alix clutched my hand, trying to reassure me.

In twenty-five minutes I was in the Park Avenue office of Dr. Mitchell Gaynor, a young, soft-spoken hematologist with a calm, reassuring manner. "I'm going to repeat the blood tests and I'll need a bone marrow biopsy," he told me as he ushered me into a large examination room with a wide table in the middle. After taking off my clothes and donning a paper robe, I climbed up on the table and lay face down. Dr. Gaynor warned me that I might feel some pain, as he injected me with a local anesthetic.

Moments later, he plunged a long needle deep into my lower back at the iliac crest of my pelvic bone, then twisted it like a corkscrew to extract the marrow he needed to confirm the diagnosis. I felt a sense of extreme pressure, and despite the anesthetic, a sharp pain shot down my leg. I shuddered at the grinding sound of metal into bone; my leg jerked involuntarily.

As he worked, Dr. Gaynor asked, "Do you have any brothers or sisters?" I told him I had two younger brothers, thinking he was making polite chitchat. He swabbed antiseptic over the biopsy site, then applied a big gauze bandage, warning me not to take it off for twenty-four hours.

Wincing as I sat down in his office afterward, I listened as he told me that he would know more in a couple of days, but was fairly sure that I had chronic myelogenous leukemia. "CML is a more indolent form of leukemia," he explained; as Dr. Marks had said, the danger was not as imminent as some of the more acute forms of the cancer, and I had several options to consider for treatment. He mentioned interferon, an immune-boosting drug he had been working with that put some patients into remission. He also mentioned a bone marrow transplant, a procedure I was only dimly aware of, as something to think about down the road. He was glad to hear I had siblings; we would need to test both my brothers to see if they could provide a "match" that would make a transplant possible.

My head was spinning as I tried to take in all that he was saying. The incongruity of it struck me as almost comic. A few hours earlier, my biggest concern had been getting my story into the paper on deadline; now I was focused on the reality that I probably had leukemia, and might need a bone marrow transplant, whatever that entailed. Would they have to suck marrow out of my bones and inject my brother's, assuming it matched? I had no clue. I wasn't even sure what bone marrow had to do with anything.

I rejoined an anxious Alix in the waiting room, and we walked to my apartment four blocks away on Ninetieth Street and Madison Avenue. The afternoon had grown colder, and we dodged children on their way home from the half-dozen schools in the neighborhood. As we parted at the entrance to my building, she begged me not to be too worried, and reminded me of the words Dr. Gaynor had said as he ushered me out of his office: "You'll be fine."

But in fact, I wasn't fine. I stayed home the next morning to wait for his call, and at 11 A.M. Dr. Gaynor called to confirm that his diagnosis was correct. I was soon to learn that this form of leukemia, indolent as it might be for now, could kill me within one to five years. Nothing would ever be the same again in my life, nor in the life of anyone who cared for me. Everything I had taken for granted—my daily concerns, my work, my well-being, my sense of my place in the world, and even my physical appearance—was about to be taken away from me. My own mortality, something I had never seriously considered, was suddenly staring me in the face.

Though I didn't know it yet, my only chance for survival would be a radical and painful therapy that was itself potentially fatal. What I *did* know was that I had to find out everything I could about the disease that had invaded me, and figure out what I could do to stop it from destroying me. I was starting from nowhere, complete ignorance. I had never before been so grateful for all my years of journalistic training. There was an investigative story here, and my life depended on getting to the bottom of it.

After absorbing the news that you have cancer, the next hardest thing is telling the people who love you. You are about to rock their lives to the foundations, and drag them along with you into this uncharted territory. There's no easy way to break news like this. Trying to keep your own emotions in check while you do it can help keep the panic level down all around. If your family thinks you are dealing with it, they will at least try to deal with it too, for your sake.

My immediate family was a tight-knit unit composed of my parents, Beverly and Sylvester Landro, and my brothers, Arthur, thirty-five, and Christopher, thirty-two. I had always thought of us as an average, happy family until I met so many people who had grown up in dysfunctional homes—then I realized just how blessed I had been. My father was cool, funny, collected, and quiet; I never even heard him raise his voice in anger. My mother, by contrast, was passionate, emotional, and enthusiastic about things. Both grew up in small towns in western Pennsylvania, my father one of nine children of Italian immigrants, and my mother an adopted only child with some Scotch-Irish roots. Thanks to the GI Bill, my dad, a veteran of two wars, got his education and a way out of what might have been a dead-end job in a coal mine. My mother, I am certain, could have become a doctor instead of a nurse had the opportunities been available to her in the 1940s.

My parents had no wealth, family connections, or friends in high places. What they did have was an unlimited reservoir of love for each other and for us, a strong sense of ethics and fairness, and a desire to see their children grow up happy and successful. They always told us that we were special, and that there was nothing we couldn't accomplish on our own if we put our minds to it. "Remember who you are," was my dad's favorite admonition.

We grew up in the middle-class suburb of Fair Lawn, New Jersey, where I graduated from high school in 1972. A few years later, when the electronics company my father worked for was sold, he decided to start his own business back in Pittsburgh, where most of our relatives still lived. There was nothing keeping him in New Jersey; Chris, the youngest, was off to college in Ohio, Art was in the Air Force and stationed in South Dakota, and I was already living and working in New York.

I still missed having my parents accessible to me in a quick trip over the George Washington Bridge, and now I had to break their hearts over the phone. On Friday, shortly after hearing from Dr. Gaynor, I dialed their number. I took a few deep breaths to try and steady my voice, worried that the minute I heard my mother's voice I might burst into tears. She answered on the second ring, delighted as usual to hear from me. "Blackie, pick up the phone, it's Laura!" she called out to my father, using the nickname that had stuck to him since World War II, when he had a thick mane of black hair. When I heard his voice on the extension, I just started talking. "Listen, please don't worry, I've got some bad news, but I'm not sure what it all means yet."

As I told them that I had been diagnosed with leukemia, my mother gasped. Recently she had become even more specialized as a nurse, going to night school for her bachelor's degree and becoming certified in oncology. In her current job, helping to run a hospice and home-care clinic for the terminally ill, she had seen some leukemia patients die. "Please don't let that ever happen to my child," she had often said to herself. Now she struggled to recover from her shock that it indeed had happened to her own daughter.

Determined not to let me see how afraid she was, she shifted into her calm, take-charge nurse mode, the trait that made my mother the best person to turn to in a real emergency. She said she would call a prominent hematologist associated with her employer, the South Hills Health System in Pittsburgh, and she asked for my doctor's phone number so she could quiz him herself.

On the extension, my father had been silent; he could barely trust himself to speak. Always of the mind that long-distance phone calls required extreme brevity, he would often call me at work, sing the first line of Stevie Wonder's "I Just Called to Say I Love You," and hang up after ascertaining that I was doing okay. Usually, when my mother and I were gabbing on the phone, he would tune in for a minute, then ring off, saying, "Talk to your mother." Now his voice broke as he said it.

After we hung up, my parents held each other and cried. "For the first time in my life, I felt as if I couldn't protect you," my dad told me much later.

Next I broke the news to my two younger brothers. They were disbelieving at first, unable to grasp that my life could be in danger. I was the glamorous, sophisticated big sister working in an office in New York, still bossing them around a little and trying to tell them how to run their lives. Nothing could happen to me; if anyone had been in harm's way, it was them—two daredevil kids who had played tough sports, gone skydiving for fun, and headed right into the military after college. By contrast, I shunned physical risk so completely that I refused to learn to ski with them when we were teenagers. They loved hiking and camping; I liked fancy hotels and shopping. They were fearless; I was scared of spiders.

But different as we were, much of what divided us growing up was simply along gender lines; they were real boys, and I was a real girl. Otherwise, we had developed the same attitudes about most things in life, we laughed at the same jokes, and we had a fierce desire to protect one another from any threat. Art was divorced, and both Chris and I were still single; with no new family units of our own, we grew even closer to one another as adults.

Both of my brothers had been largely influenced by my dad, a proponent of military service. Art signed up for ROTC during college, then spent five years as an Air Force officer in the Strategic Air Command. Now he was working for a telecommunications company in Connecticut, traveling frequently to Europe and South America on business. Chris had just completed a five-year stint as a Marine officer, including a full tour of duty in the Persian Gulf War. After his discharge, he landed a job in Ohio working for the Anchor-Hocking Glass division of Newell Corp., a diversified manufacturing company. Both were still active in the reserves, doing their weekend-warrior thing once a month and spending two weeks a year on active duty.

The worst crisis our family had faced up until the day I was diagnosed with leukemia was the Persian Gulf War. During the seven months that Chris was stationed there, we lived our lives around CNN reports from Operation Desert Storm, trying to reassure one another that nothing would happen to him. I watched CNN all day on the small television in my office and turned it on again as soon as I came home from work, often staying up until 2 A.M. to catch the latest developments.

A few times, after a particularly terrifying report on casualties or a bombing, the phone would ring, and it would be Chris. I would be thinking about him so hard I was sure the call was the result of telepathy. But of course it was really one benefit of modern telecommunications: he knew CNN was broadcasting every minute of the war, and he was usually able to make it to some phone line to let us know he was okay when he needed to.

After he returned safely, the family was able to relax, sure that having had him in the path of Scud missiles was the worst thing we were all going to have to deal with for a very long time. But when I spoke to Chris on the phone, he told me we had to approach what was happening to me as a war too, and we must fight it just as hard. "This is just another line of Iraqi defenses we didn't expect," he said.

I was soon to find out how completely dependent on my family I was. All of them would put their lives on hold—and even at risk—to help save mine. We had always relied on love and a sense of humor to get us through everything. Even in hard times, we always found something to laugh about. "So, they could still call and say this was all a mistake, right?" Chris kept asking in an attempt to get a laugh out of me. But I couldn't laugh—this was no mistake.

If I knew my family was with me, I was less certain about what would happen to the life I had made for myself in New York. I had no time to worry about leukemia; I was busy, at the peak of my career. I loved getting up in the morning and racing down to work to see what might happen that day. I had stories to write, reporters to manage, trips to take.

Besides, I had not even started to do all the other important things in life, like get married and have a family of my own. True, my biological clock was ticking away, but it wasn't too late for me, as I often told myself. Many of the women of my generation who spent their twenties and early thirties building a career were now having kids in their late thirties and even their early forties, helped by fertility drugs if need be.

But suddenly time wasn't on my side anymore. I surveyed my personal life with some dismay. Over the previous decade, I had always had a boyfriend, but most of my relationships lasted one to two years and then ended when it was clear there was nothing resembling a future there. One former boyfriend told me he thought his parents' terrible marriage had damaged his chances for being in a successful one himself. But he warned me that I might be at an equal disadvantage because my parents' strong and loving marriage had led me to have unrealistic expectations. I wasn't buying this. I still held out hope that some day I would find my true soulmate, the love of my life.

But if he was out there, I certainly hadn't had much luck finding him. My current relationship was with an attorney seven years my senior, whom I had started seeing in February 1990. Though we cared for each other, it was becoming clear that we didn't share the same goals in life or get excited about the same things. We had already talked several times about breaking up and moving on with our lives. Though we were living together, I still had kept my own apartment, and was preparing to move back to it.

Though he had been supportive and concerned the night after my appointment with Dr. Gaynor, doing his best to keep me as calm as possible and volunteering to do anything he could to help, after I got the firm diagnosis of leukemia, I was prepared for things to end between us. The last thing I needed was the further strain and ambivalence of an uncommitted relationship. I wanted to make it easy for him to just go away. "You didn't bargain for this," I told him. "But I have to focus all my energy on getting through it, and I fully understand if you want out."

To my surprise, he had the opposite reaction. After coming home from work the next day, Friday, October 25, he sat down in the chair opposite me without even taking off his raincoat. "I love you, and I think we should try to get through this together," he said to me. "Let's get married." I was stunned. It was the last thing I expected him to say. But just the fact that he was saying it had an enormous effect on me. I was in a complete crisis, and he was reaching out his hand to me. "Are you sure?" I asked. "Do you want twenty-four hours to think it over?" He had thought it over; he was sure. I felt a rush of love, relief, and gratitude, and my concerns about the relationship seemed to dissolve instantly. I said yes.

We called my family, still reeling from the news of my disease, to tell them that we were engaged. They were happy for me, as well as surprised, for they too had not expected the relationship to last. It gave us something positive and life-affirming to focus on, a sign of hope, of planning for the future. I didn't want anyone to look on me with pity. Over the weekend, as we began to tell friends about both our marriage and my illness, I would try to be droll, opening with, "We have good news and bad news."

I asked my best friend, Nancy Kaufman, to help me plan a wedding and be my maid of honor. We had been inseparable since grade school in Fair Lawn, where she lived down the block from me. We met our first boyfriends, smoked our first cigarettes, and hung out at the first shopping malls together. We attended the same summer camps and took cross-country trips together. We had cried on each other's shoulders and been chief counsel on every important decision in each other's lives. Nearly thirty years later, she was the person I knew I could call and wake up at 2 A.M. if I had to talk about something.

Nancy lived farther downtown from me now instead of farther down the block, and our hangouts had become more upscale. Instead of meeting at the mall in Jersey, we hooked up these days on Fifth Avenue. The Saturday after my diagnosis, I asked her to meet me for lunch at Bergdorf Goodman. As we sipped cappuccinos in the department store's seventh-floor café, she begged me to forget about a wedding, worried that it would exhaust me, that I might get sicker before I could pull it off. "If you are really going to go through with this, why don't you just go down to City Hall and have a quick ceremony?" she urged me. But I was determined to be a real bride. I wanted it all: the white dress, the flowers, the vows: "Till death do us part."

Families and friends are the ones you usually know you can rely on in a health crisis; it is much more daunting to contemplate the impact it will have on your professional life. After fifteen years as a journalist, ten of them at *The Wall Street Journal,* I suddenly felt as if everything I had worked for was in jeopardy. Learning you have cancer during the most productive years of your career is like having trained for a marathon for years, pacing yourself at a brisk clip, and then suddenly being sidelined by a freak injury while the other runners pass you by. In most cases, you have no choice but to step out of the race and then to reconnoiter if you ever hope to get back in it.

My first exposure to the newspaper business came in the third grade, after a school trip to our local paper, *The Bergen Record*. Afterward, my class began publishing *The Little Record,* a mimeographed sheet full of school news, and I was the news editor. Later, as typical of many others in my generation, I was inspired by the example of Bob Woodward and Carl Bernstein, and majored in journalism at Ohio University. In my senior year, after an internship at *The Pittsburgh Press* and two years on the college paper, I wrote letters to dozens of newspapers. I got one job offer: a starting reporter's job at *The Hartford Courant* in Connecticut, covering one of the outlying towns in its readership area.

At about the same time, however, I won an internship to work in London, one of five such internships at overseas news-gathering organizations handed out by John Wilhelm, the director of the communications program at Ohio University. *The Hartford Courant* told me I had to take their job right now if I wanted it. But I wasn't about to give up an internship in London, however temporary, to cover sewer and water hearings in some Connecticut town.

That decision more or less set me on the path toward business journalism, since the London internship was with McGraw-Hill World News, which provided stories and background information to a group of trade magazines, newsletters, and wire service reports. I had barely squeaked through Economics 101 in college, and suddenly I found myself reporting on the oil industry, the metal trading business, nuclear power companies, and petrochemical trading. Surprisingly I found I actually liked it; I was soon flying up to visit oil rigs in the North Sea, covering Energy Department press conferences, and traveling all over Europe to report stories.

My internship stretched out for almost a year, and then one of the newsletters back in New York that I had been reporting for on the nuclear energy industry offered me a job. It entailed more international traveling, reporting on nuclear nonproliferation talks and International Atomic Energy Agency conferences, and on the battles among environmentalists, uranium miners and processors, and nuclear power plant operators. Two years later, after paying my dues in the trenches of trade reporting, I landed a job at McGraw-Hill's flagship publication, *BusinessWeek* magazine.

Finally I was working for a publication that people I knew had heard of, but I still yearned to work for a newspaper. Two years later, I found the perfect employer: *The Wall Street Journal.* The country's largest newspaper, it was then expanding its domain, adding social, political, and consumer-oriented coverage to its focus on traditional businesses such as steel, autos, manufacturing, and finance. In 1981, just after I turned twenty-seven, I was hired to cover a fast-growing new beat—telecommunications, cable TV, and entertainment.

My job kept me shuttling between New York and Los Angeles, reporting on Hollywood studios that were flush with new growth from videocassettes, cable, and expanding foreign markets. There were endless tales of corporate intrigue, clashes among the big egos who ran the entertainment companies, and a steady parade of megadeals and mergers to write about.

I started a gradual shift into management a few years later, when the *Journal* started a special "Media and Marketing" page with a dozen reporters under a bright, respected young editor named John Andrew. In addition to reporting and writing my own stories, I helped him edit stories by the other reporters. Tragically, John died after a brief illness a couple of years later, and I was asked to take over the group. I agreed to the assignment, but insisted on continuing to report and write my own stories, which my editors were only too happy to oblige. It would mean a lot more work, but though I had managerial ambitions, I wasn't ready to give up my byline.

Because I had set my sights on being Superwoman, it was with considerable trepidation that I called my editors at the *Journal* to tell them I had been grounded. Would they start to worry about my ability to handle my job, I wondered; would they start thinking about replacing me? These were all completely natural fears—no matter how beneficent an organization is, things *do* have to keep going. I asked Paul Steiger, the managing editor, to meet with me on the afternoon of Thursday, October 31. A week earlier he had gotten wind that something was wrong with me, having heard it from the national news editor, Marty Schenker, on the day I had to leave the office.

As I sat down with him, I was trembling from the effort of trying to remain composed. I described the situation, trying to downplay its seriousness. But I had to tell him the truth: I was seriously ill and expected to need time off, perhaps several months, to deal with it. "The most important thing I need to know is that you'll support me, that everything will be okay if I have to leave for a while," I said. I tried to be funny, adding, "Think of it as a maternity leave, only with no baby."

Paul was unequivocal in assuring me that my job would be waiting for me when I returned. But he and Norman Pearlstine, then the paper's executive editor, went even further, offering to talk to top management and benefits executives to make sure I had everything I needed. As I left that meeting with Paul, though, I fought back tears, wanting to be thought of as I always had been: tough, strong, on top of it.

In my fear, I had underestimated the paper's regard for me, as well as my editors' concern and generosity. There was a strong paternal culture at the paper—they took care of their own in a crisis. In talking to others who have been through similar situations, I found that many companies, despite their rules and outlines for medical emergencies, disability leaves, and the like, will make special accommodations for a sick employee. Coworkers will work overtime to cover for a colleague who is ill; managers can bend the rules or put the pressure on the bean counters to do so.

When I was first diagnosed, the era of managed care was just beginning, and Dow Jones, the *Journal*'s parent company, was self-insured, which basically meant that if Aetna, the insurance company administering our plan, said no to something, Dow Jones could overrule and say yes. In my case they would do this time and again. David Rosenberg, in our employee benefits department, would soon become one of my closest allies, running interference for me with the insurance company whenever I needed help.

Word of my illness started to leak out pretty fast around the office. Reporters are masters of gossip and in-house intrigue; there was always a buzz about someone or another around the *Journal,* and now it was me. One by one my reporters started drifting into my office, some awkwardly, some bluntly asking me to explain what was wrong. It had been just two years since they lost a young boss to an untimely death, and no one could believe such misfortune might strike our group twice in a row. Years of watching my aggressive style had persuaded them I was indestructible. "Not you, Laura," Meg Cox, one of my reporters, insisted when I explained the situation. "Something like this couldn't happen to you . . . you're invincible!"

Before I even had time to tell some of my good friends at other parts of the paper, they heard the news through the grapevine. One afternoon, Julie Salamon, the *Journal*'s movie reviewer, knocked on my office door, a stricken look on her face. She sat down and said, "Laura, is this true? Do you have leukemia?" She told me she had been at a party the night before where she heard the news from other *Journal* colleagues. "I'm sorry to say it is true," I told her, trying to hide my growing paranoia that I was being gossiped about.

Though angry and defensive at first, I soon realized there was no use getting upset. When it strikes close to home, cancer is big news, even in an organization like the *Journal;* people have to talk about it. For some, talking directly to the victim is difficult; they don't know what to say or how to act. But there is no use trying to hide from coworkers the fact that one has cancer. One good outcome of being open is that people want to help. And that is where some of the best help will come from. Within a few days of my diagnosis I had a dozen friends both inside and outside *The Wall Street Journal* offering introductions to expert doctors, volunteering connections all over the place, and putting me in touch with people they knew who had been through similar health problems.

That kind of networking can prove invaluable. Joining the ranks of the afflicted is almost like joining a secret society or a special fraternity. Other members want to reach out to you, to share their experiences and put you in touch with the experts who helped them. If you find yourself in a similar position, take them up on it. Only those who have been there really know what you are going through and can offer you the proof that there is hope, that you can come out on the other side, alive and well.

One person I turned to for assistance was Michael Waldholz, the *Journal's* senior medical writer. "Mike, I need whatever you have, anyone you know who I can talk to about leukemia," I told him as we sat in my office the week after Dr. Gaynor's diagnosis. By the next day, he produced a stack of papers, medical journals and textbooks, and a list of phone numbers of top specialists he knew. Though he urged me to educate myself as thoroughly as possible, he cautioned me that the task of researching my disease and its treatment would be daunting, and that understanding medical jargon as a layperson would be frustrating. "You are entering the netherworld of medicine," he warned.

He had that right. In that world, I would be given conflicting and sometimes incomprehensible advice. I would soon learn as much about the politics of different centers that treated leukemia as I would learn about the different treatments themselves. I would learn about the most intricate details of bone marrow transplantation, a constantly shifting science with several methodologies that several major centers had a different approach to. In the months to come, I would have to make decisions about complex medical matters even while in the throes of a life-threatening sickness. If I was wrong, I could be dead wrong. But it would be up to me in the end: I had to take charge of my own care.

Acting strong and in control actually helped me feel tougher—the old "whistle a happy tune" scenario—and sometimes I even amazed myself at how well I seemed to be dealing with everything. But I had to fight every day to ward off the despair I felt inside. It helped to organize everything, to gather documents as if I really were reporting a story. I kept copious notes on everything, and amassed thick folders to keep track of everything I was learning about CML. As I took notes on things like blood counts and disease progression, I found it helped to write down my feelings and my fears as well.

"I careen between optimism and certainty that I will beat this, and absolute certainty that I won't," I wrote a week after I was diagnosed. "I must for the first time in my life bend my will toward believing that something that could go either way will in fact go my way. The best thing I can manage so far is a sort of suppression or denial. Even as I am doing all the right things I know I have to do—the calls, the doctor visits, the research, the organization—inside I know I am not dealing with it . . . it just hasn't sunk in yet. Maybe for now that is all I can deal with, all I can countenance. Take it a day, a week at a time." Denial can be a very important part of dealing with cancer—as long as what you are denying is the possibility of death.

And in the first few days that I knew I had leukemia, I would wake up in the middle of the night, thinking I could feel the blood running amuck in my veins, the marrow churning out renegade cells in my bones. I would envision white cells zooming out like quicksilver, and try to will them to stop. In one of my darkest moments, I brooded that by Darwin's measure, I wasn't destined to survive. My body had randomly been programmed to self-destruct about halfway through a normal lifespan.

But one night, as I reflected about what a flawed specimen I had turned out to be, I began to feel angry, even rebellious. Nothing was going to take me down so fast—I just wasn't going to let it happen. Darwin's theory needed a new interpretation, one that worked for me. Survival of the fittest for me would mean using all the information and technology available to find out how to beat this disease; it would mean taking advantage of all that modern medicine offered if I hoped to outfox death. I would defy destiny with science. I was determined to survive.

DOWN TO
THE MARROW

Fifteen years as a reporter had taught me that the key to getting the story was in asking the right questions, the right way, of the right source. And I had learned that the only way to figure out the right questions was to do my homework beforehand. Knowledge, while terrifying, is power. If you are informed, you can't be patronized, intimidated, or pushed around by the health care system.

Dr. Gaynor told me I had time, perhaps as much as a year, before the disease might advance to a dangerous stage. There was a drug called hydroxy urea that could help control my white blood cell production, but once I started taking the drug, it was only a matter of time before its effectiveness decreased. He suggested holding off at least for a few weeks, since my blood counts were fairly stable. I was to visit him once a week on my way to work for a blood test and physical exam to monitor the disease's progress.

Though Dr. Gaynor gave me some pamphlets about leukemia and bone marrow transplants, what was available in 1991 was elementary and simplistic. (There is much more information available to patients today on the Internet, through Web sites such as the University of Pennsylvania's Oncolink.) I knew I would have to dig much deeper to find out everything I could about the progression of chronic leukemia, the science of bone marrow transplantation,

and the alternative treatments. My mother consulted Dr. Robert
Hilberg, the hematological oncologist who was the director of the
hospice where she worked, and he agreed to act as a sounding
board for us, answering the questions that came up as we combed
through medical studies and spoke to other experts. But he also
gave her some advice we all needed: don't project the worst; focus
on the real possibility of a cure. It was the simplest, yet most important, advice we could get. We had to believe that I was going to be
cured, because the alternative was just not acceptable.

As I thought about who else I might be able to recruit for my research team, I called on my friend of nearly fifteen years, Marilyn
Dammerman. We met in 1976 in London, when I had just graduated from college and was working as an intern at McGraw-Hill.
She was then a reporter at *Forbes* magazine's London bureau, but
she was frequently on the road doing a story. I needed a place to
live, and when she was in town, she often stayed with her
boyfriend, a scientist, so she was more than happy to have a room-
mate to help pay the rent on the flat she was rarely in. When she
had spare time, we might have dinner together at a local Indian
restaurant, or just explore London together.

The London boyfriend didn't last, but Marilyn's interest in the
science he exposed her to did. A few years later, after moving back
to the United States, she left journalism to go back to school and
earn a doctorate in biomedical science. Now she was a full-fledged
scientist herself, working in a lab at Rockefeller University, a prominent research university in New York. Though our worlds had
sharply diverged and the demands of her work left her little time
for socializing, we always stayed in touch. Marilyn, one of the most
intense, driven people I have ever met, had married a warm, easy-
going physician, Noah Robbins, who was an infectious disease specialist at Montefiore Hospital in the Bronx.

We still shared our passion for spicy food, and every couple of
months we'd have dinner at a Thai or Indian restaurant and catch

up on each other's lives. I would ask her to explain her gene research, trying to follow what she was saying as she excitedly described her lab work delving into the hereditary basis of blood
triglyceride levels. On November 7, my fiancé and I met Noah and
Marilyn for dinner at our favorite Indian restaurant, Dawat, on
East Fifty-eighth Street. I had already briefed Marilyn on the phone
with all I knew about my condition. They promised to do whatever
they could to help.

Marilyn would prove to be my secret weapon in this war.
Though leukemia was way outside her field, the combination of her
journalism background, her scientific knowledge, and her awesome
ability to focus on a project would ultimately help point me in the
right direction and force me to confront the difficult decisions that
could save my life.

This was just before the Internet revolution opened up the
floodgates on medical information to the average person. Through
Rockefeller, however, Marilyn had access to a medical library and
the online service called Medline, which was the electronic link to
the National Institutes of Health. Now easily available to anyone
with a computer, a modem, and a Web browser, as are numerous
other medical-information sites, Medline was a gold mine of information and abstracts summarizing papers from all over the world
on CML. She was able to pull up abstracts of the most relevant clinical papers and studies, all with the latest research in the field. Marilyn would fax papers to me at the office, underlining important
parts or conclusions, scribbling little notes to explain things I might
not understand. My fiancé, who had a keen analytical mind, would
pore over the statistical aspects of the papers, discussing survival
rates for the disease under various kinds of treatment.

In November, I went to work every day, staying late at the office
to hunt around the databases myself. With the computer I used to
write and edit stories, I could access hundreds of publications
through my company's Dow Jones News Retrieval electronic

archive service. I found stories that had been written on leukemia, many in laymen's terms, that were based on scientific studies. I cold-called many of the prominent leukemia specialists and researchers whose names appeared on studies that Marilyn sent or that I turned up, and Mike Waldholz made calls to introduce me to those scientists he knew personally.

Though the idea of cold-calling a doctor or scientist sounds daunting, most of them were accessible, ready to spend a few minutes on the phone with someone who had read their research. Of course, the problem with understanding something enough to ask an intelligent question is that it is like knowing enough of a foreign language to ask directions: the person you've asked usually assumes you are proficient and answers you in detail, speaking so fast you don't understand a word of it. Though I tried to absorb as much as I could of what these experts said, I often had to tape the conversations with doctors so I could listen to them again later.

Searching for the cause of my disease, I soon learned, was pointless. Family history wasn't considered a factor in leukemia. The only known external causes of the disease were exposure to nuclear radiation or toxic petrochemicals such as benzene. Survivors of atomic disasters at Nagasaki and Hiroshima had a high incidence of the disease, as did more recent victims of nuclear accidents like Chernobyl. Some people who had been treated with radiation for other cancers developed CML later. Though I covered the nuclear industry for two years and toured a few reactors and uranium mines, that hardly qualified as exposure to radiation. Over the years I'd had my share of X rays at the dentist, but that was about it.

My mother worried that maybe I had been exposed to electromagnetic waves; when I was an infant we lived for a short time in a New Jersey town crisscrossed by high-tension electrical wires. And I had been sitting in front of a computer at work many hours a week for almost ten years. But while we read plenty of theories and studies indicating such exposure could trigger a reaction in the body's cells that would lead to leukemia, most concluded that there was no absolute proof.

As I read the basic facts about leukemia, I was amazed at my ignorance of my own body, and I found myself wishing I had paid more attention in biology class. I never knew bone marrow did anything except sit in your bones; for all I knew, the only use for marrow was to be found in the recipe for osso bucco, made with veal bones. But I learned, in fact, that the spongy substance inside bones contains stem cells, the fundamental units that are responsible for the immune system and the production of blood cells. Bone marrow makes white cells to fight infection, red cells to carry oxygen and remove waste products from organs and tissues, and the platelets that enable the blood to clot. In healthy adults, the marrow produces 100 million red cells and 400 million white cells per hour, with the mature cells lasting only a few days or months.

But in people like me who develop leukemia, the system breaks down for reasons no one completely understands. The stem cells in the marrow malfunction, and some blood cells fail to properly mature, stalling at an early stage of development and self-replicating uncontrollably. People with my version of the disease, chronic myelogenous leukemia, almost always have a specific chromosomal abnormality that activates an "oncogene" that causes the marrow to start overproducing white blood cells. The abnormality was called the Philadelphia chromosome, and tests showed that I had it. It seemed unfair to have a bad gene named for the much-maligned city of Philadelphia.

How long had this condition been active in me? Impossible to say. My most recent prior blood test was during a vacation in the summer of 1990, when sharp chest pains sent me to the emergency room at Southampton Hospital on Long Island. The diagnosis was pleurisy, an inflammation of the lining of a lung. Nothing abnormal had been evident in the blood test they took at the time.

So luckily, my disease had been caught fairly early, in what they call "first chronic phase." A patient can have the chronic form of leukemia for years without any major symptoms. Before doctors began routine blood testing, CML was often very advanced when it was finally diagnosed. But as in my case, symptoms do eventually begin to surface. The spleen, the organ in the upper abdomen that makes other types of white blood cells and filters out old blood cells, becomes engorged with white cells—that had been the source of the nagging pain in my side. Fatigue, which I had, and night sweats, which I had also experienced, often follow.

Eventually, CML progresses to an accelerated, and then a "blast" phase. At that point, dysfunctional blast cells start to replace everything else in the blood. The white blood cell count soars higher, and the disease begins to look like the more deadly form, acute leukemia. The rest is total devastation: the immune system is destroyed, bacterial and fungal infections attack the patient, and, three to six months later, you die. If the infections aren't the killer, death can come from a massive internal hemorrhage or a flood of external bleeding. "You can even have a fatal nosebleed," one researcher I talked to told me. "It can be pretty horrible."

Of course, Gaynor, my cheerful hematologist, accentuated the positive: I was in an early chronic phase; there were plenty of things to do, and I had months, even a year to decide what was best. He was initially leaning toward recommending a course of interferon, a chemical used to boost the body's own ability to fight cancer. But I wasn't encouraged by what I was reading about interferon. One expert on the drug told me that interferon might at best put me into a form of remission; it was the best option if a patient had no donor for a bone marrow transplant.

A transplant, I learned, was much different and more complicated from what I had envisioned. There was no actual surgery involved for me; that bone marrow of mine that was making the errant blood cells would have to be destroyed through chemotherapy and radiation. But if I was lucky enough to have a compatible donor, that person—probably one of my brothers—would be the one to undergo surgery. Needles would be drilled into his hip bones to extract a small amount of healthy marrow, which would then be given to me intravenously, like a blood transfusion.

In a meeting with my fiancé and me in early November, Dr. Gaynor told us of several transplant centers, mentioning the Fred Hutchinson Cancer Center in Seattle, Washington, whose transplant team had won a Nobel Prize for its pioneering work in the field. "Seattle!?" I said. "Forget it! Why should I have to go 3,000 miles away from home for months of medical treatment?" I was in New York, after all, the capital of everything. "Well, then you can go to Memorial," Dr. Gaynor said, referring to world-renowned Memorial Sloan-Kettering Cancer Center on East Sixty-eighth Street and First Avenue.

Back at the office, I asked Mike Waldholz if he knew anyone there, and he put me in touch with Dr. David Golde, who had recently left the medical center of the University of California at Los Angeles to head Sloan-Kettering's hematological oncology department. After making an appointment to see him, I searched through the computerized archives for some background information on him. I find it's best to know as much as you can about a doctor before you meet him, particularly if the physician has recently changed jobs. Usually a doctor will switch for a better opportunity or promotion, but sometimes you might learn something about a doctor's background that can help you evaluate him or her as a professional and get a sense of what kind of person you are dealing with.

Searching the databases for Golde's name, I came up with a flood of entries, including a few references to a letter Golde had written urging a lighter sentence for convicted junk bond king Michael Milken because of all he had done for cancer research. Then I came across dozens of headlines, such as one that read

"COURT BACKS DOCTOR'S RIGHT TO USE PATIENT'S TISSUES," in the *Los Angeles Times*.

As I browsed through the articles, I learned that Golde had been embroiled for years in a lawsuit with a former patient whose cancerous spleen he had removed. Though the operation appeared to have saved the patient's life, he sued after learning that Golde had used his liberated spleen and some of his blood cells—without informing him or asking permission—to develop an anticancer drug. Golde received a windfall from the drug, and the patient, John Moore, had contended that he deserved a share of the profits. A state court agreed that a patient's tissues and blood remained his property even after they were removed from his body.

The case had gone all the way to the Supreme Court, generating plenty of controversy and debate along the way. Some saw it as a financial threat to the burgeoning biotechnology field, and to scientists who were genetically altering human cells to produce all kinds of new drugs and treatments for cancer and other diseases. The California State Supreme Court overturned the decision, and finally, the U.S. Supreme Court refused to hear an appeal from Mr. Moore, handing Golde and UCLA a victory.

Some of the most interesting commentary on the lawsuit came from people who admired Dr. Golde's research and praised his drug discovery, yet still found something unsavory about the whole thing. In an editorial in *The Washington Post*, Frank Swoboda, who had suffered from the same disease as Mr. Moore, excoriated Golde and UCLA for their lack of candor with Mr. Moore, finding "something sleazy" about the fact that they never told the patient what they were up to.

And plenty of others criticized the way UCLA had arranged for Mr. Moore to continue coming to Los Angeles from his home in Seattle twice a year for seven years. The hospital went so far as to pay his airfare and put him up in a posh Beverly Hills hotel without ever telling him that what he thought was follow-up care was largely a way for UCLA to keep tapping his bodily tissues. As the headline of one *San Francisco Examiner* article I found put it, "MAN'S SPLEEN GETS TAKEN FOR A RIDE." As for Golde, I couldn't wait to meet this guy.

On November 4, as I waited with my fiancé in Golde's office, I saw a letter from my hematologist and my medical chart spread out on his desk. Using my reporter's well-honed ability to decipher something upside down, I skimmed over the summary on my condition. According to medical lingo, I was ". . . a well-appearing female in no acute distress." That seemed like an odd way to describe me, but I guess it was true: I looked okay, and I wasn't desperately ill. Yet as the letter went on to say, I was indeed quite ill: ". . . findings consistent with chronic myelogenous leukemia." The letter noted that I had "denied radiation exposure."

At that point, Golde burst in. Robust, fair-haired, and pleasant-looking, he had an air of good-natured self-confidence and that preternatural cheerfulness one often encounters in people who have spent a lot of time on the West Coast. We chitchatted a few minutes about the merits of L.A. versus New York life, and he asked me how I felt when I was diagnosed. I told him I was still having trouble believing it.

"You're a very healthy lady with CML," he told me. He advised me to try to achieve some kind of "detachment" from my disease, and to try and transcend it, telling me a parable about an Indian hunter and a captured parrot, which I didn't quite follow. He told me to draw on my "philosophic reserves." I replied that my philosophy was that I was going to beat this. "That's good!" he boomed.

I couldn't help liking Dr. Golde, and I could see how he could charm someone out of his or her bodily fluids if he wanted to. But just as I was beginning to wonder if he had any actual medical advice for me, he got down to business. He was unequivocal in rejecting the idea of interferon. "Short of transplantation, there is no known cure," Golde advised me. "You should undergo a transplant as soon as possible if one of your two brothers is a match."

Golde admitted the transplant was a harrowing and dangerous procedure, confirming everything I had read and lending support to all my fears. Though I would enter the hospital for a bone marrow transplant with a functioning immune system and a normal appearance, once inside all that would change. I would be bombarded with near-lethal doses of chemotherapy and enough radiation to destroy my bone marrow and to completely knock out my immune system. Then, when I was as close to dead as possible, I would be given an intravenous infusion of marrow from my donor. But even that might not be the end because even if the marrow was a match, it might be rejected.

Assuming I didn't die right away from rejection, for weeks, even months after that, I would be subject to life-threatening infections, with no immune system yet reestablished to fight them. And even marrow that was a perfect match—the same combination of genetic material as my own—could trigger a bad reaction from my body. Because the donor's marrow, known as the graft, could recognize that my body was not its own, the immune system cells in the donor marrow might attack me, the host. They even had a name for it—"graft-versus-host disease"—and it could kill you.

But if the transplant worked, the marrow would take, or "engraft," start sprouting new marrow free of disease, and grow a whole new immune system. The leukemia would go away, it was hoped, never to return. Before we did anything else, Golde said, we needed to test my brothers. For a transplant to be successful, certain genetic markers, known as human leukocyte antigens, or HLA, had to match each other in donor and patient as closely as possible. Every human has six of these antigens, three from each parent, that are critical for a match. A person's HLA type is like a cellular identification card. The only sure bet for a match was an identical twin; otherwise, no matter how many siblings in a family, there is about a

one-in-four chance that any one sibling will be an exact match for
any other. It was perfectly conceivable that you could have ten siblings and still have no match. The odds were daunting.

According to a report to Congress on bone marrow transplantation prepared by the General Accounting Office, two-thirds of the
patients who might have benefited from a bone marrow transplant
between 1987 and 1991 had no related donor with compatible tissues. For the ones with no related match, the only hope was using
an unrelated compatible donor, a technique first tried in 1979.

Since HLA combinations are genetically inherited, they tend to
follow racial and ethnic lines. Thus I might have found someone
with similar Italian, Irish, and Scottish ancestry whose tissue
looked enough like mine to provide a compatible match. I came
across a lot of data in my research about the search for unrelated
matches, and though it was like finding a needle in a haystack, the
efforts being made were impressive.

With bone marrow transplantation offering the only possible
cure for tens of thousands of people diagnosed with leukemia and
related blood diseases, Congress authorized the establishment of a
national registry of volunteer donors, and in 1986, the U.S. Navy
funded the National Marrow Donor Program through a contract
with the American Red Cross and two blood bank associations to
broaden the pool of donors. There was also an international registry.

But as of July 1991, there were only half a million people in that
registry who were prepared to donate marrow if they matched a
needy patient. And according to the General Accounting Office,
only about 13 percent of the searches made between 1986 and 1991
to identify an initial list of potential donors ended up finding one
that resulted in a transplant.

Many patients became activists while searching for a donor.
Louisville, Kentucky, stockbroker Bill Tafel, diagnosed at age
thirty-six with CML, was one of six siblings, but not one was a

match. After seventeen potential donors in the National Marrow Donor registry proved on further testing to be unsuitable, he began his own personal campaign to broaden the pool of bone marrow donors. He helped organize local drives for a teenage girl who needed a transplant, spoke at churches and town meetings, and gave interviews to local newspapers and TV stations about the need for donors.

Tafel pestered the local Red Cross chapter to inform their platelet donors that they could be marrow donors, which they eventually agreed to do, and at one point he even went to Washington, D.C., and talked his way in to see Red Cross chief Elizabeth Dole to personally lobby the cause. Then one day, he got the word that there might be a match for him, a woman in France. Two weeks later, the match was confirmed and Tafel was on his way to the Fred Hutchinson Cancer Center in Seattle for a transplant. Today he is free of the disease.

For me, I knew my best hope was for a match from either Art or Chris. Both of my brothers' blood would have to be tested, cross-tested against my parents, and tested again to determine if there was a match among us. This was a complicated procedure that required blood to be shipped from labs in Columbus, where Chris lived, and Pittsburgh, my parents' home. Art, close by in Connecticut, could come into New York City. It was tough to coordinate it all; at one point Chris drove sixty miles to a lab in Ohio only to be told they couldn't draw his blood without a prescription, which he didn't have.

Two days after my meeting with Dr. Golde, on Wednesday, November 6, I decided to register officially as an outpatient with Sloan-Kettering's transplant unit. I took extra care with my appearance that day, donning a tailored business suit and high heels. But when I got off the elevator on the third floor of Sloan-Kettering's main building, my confidence faded. I looked around at the ashen faces of other patients, mostly dressed in rumpled jogging suits or casual clothes, many bald or with a few wisps of hair. A pallor of despair seemed to hang over the place. The technicians and staffers were efficient, but silent and unsmiling.

"I'm not one of these people!" I wanted to shout.

But I was, no matter how I tried not to look like one. I sat in front of a clerk named Darren who entered my information into the computer (father's name; mother's maiden name; who to call in an emergency; payment by credit card or check) and issued me a patient card that I was to show every time I returned there. Sent to another floor to take a chest X ray, I had my first taste of this hospital's brand of care: patients were literally lined up on stretchers in the hallways waiting their turn, like planes coming in for a landing on a foggy day at Kennedy Airport. One elderly, hairless man, frustrated at being seemingly abandoned, started wailing loudly until an orderly came to take him away. The scene was surreal, like something out of a bad Fellini movie. This was the netherworld of medicine all right.

The next day, I spent most of the morning running around personally retrieving my own bone marrow and blood slides from one lab at Sloan-Kettering and delivering them to another. The floor to which I was sent to find my slides had no receptionist, so I wandered around until I found a room full of people looking into microscopes. I told a woman there my name and she handed me my bone marrow slides in a neat little package which I carefully put in my purse. She sent me to another floor to ask for my blood samples, and I waited in an empty corridor for a half hour until another woman handed me those. I felt like I was walking around in some enemy territory with my own little death warrants.

The first tests done on Art's and Chris's blood samples were inconclusive, which was maddening. Edgy and worried, I called my brothers and asked them to come to New York so all our blood could be drawn together in one location, at one time. "Gee, I think I'm busy this weekend," was Art's attempt to get me to lighten up a little.

I still had my own apartment on East Eightieth Street, which my brothers often used as their New York crash pad. On Thursday night, we all stayed there so we could be at Sloan-Kettering first thing Friday morning. After dinner at a local Italian restaurant, Art took my arm as we walked back to the apartment. "I think Chris is going to come through for you," he told me quietly.

I instinctively knew why he thought so: our younger brother and I looked more alike, and we had developed a special bond during the time Chris had lived with me after college and before applying to Marine Corps Officer Candidate School. Still, I loved both my brothers equally, and the next morning as we walked over to Sloan-Kettering's blood drawing lab at Sixty-eighth Street and First Avenue, I felt as if I were the little sister, and that Art and Chris, suddenly older, were going to take care of me now. We arrived about 9 A.M., and sat close together in the crowded waiting room.

Chris had a noon flight back to Columbus and the plan was for Art to drop him off at La Guardia Airport and then head back up to Connecticut. Our very different personalities were soon in evidence—as usual, my brothers were completely calm and collected, while I was exhibiting mounting impatience with how long it was taking to get started. We were finally ushered back to a room with several reclining chairs that looked like Barcaloungers, and as we settled into them, I kept reminding the slow-moving technicians that my brother had a plane to catch.

The process of drawing six tubes of blood from each of us was a slow one, and they weren't about to make it any faster. We were also supposed to relax, drink juice, and eat little snacks to restore us. Though I had been outwardly in control of my emotions in almost every doctor's office I had been in up till now, this seemed to be the day I was going to freak out. When the blood was finally drawn, my brothers had about a half hour to get back to their car at Eightieth Street, and then to the airport.

As they tried to soothe me, I was growing increasingly agitated over whether they would make it on time, and fretted that they would get killed driving ninety miles an hour so Chris could catch his plane. "Relax, we're going to be fine," Chris told me as they headed out the door. In fact, they started running as soon as they left the hospital, and boasted later that they made it to La Guardia in a record time of twelve minutes. Chris got onto the plane just as the doors were about to close.

But I knew I wasn't getting hysterical about Chris missing a plane. This was my first chance to vent, an opportunity to lose control over the small stuff because I couldn't stop to contemplate the real terror. What I was really crying about was something else: the fear that neither of my brothers would provide a match, that I would sicken and die, that there was no hope, that my life was over. For the first time I realized how bleak the situation would be if neither brother could save me.

My brother Art privately wondered at that point how I would ever get through what lay ahead. "I just didn't think you would be able to handle it," he confided later.

But going ballistic about small things can help release the steam that builds up when the larger fears seem overwhelming, even incomprehensible. And once you express your fear, it's easier to find ways to psych yourself up for the time when you will really need all your courage. Talking to my mother later on the phone, she reminded me of how I once bucked her up when Chris was in the Persian Gulf. "No bad vibes, Mom, no thoughts that anything bad could ever happen; don't for an instant acknowledge that he could be hurt, only positive energy," I would tell her, trying to convince myself as well.

Though generally that kind of talk wasn't like me, that was the mind-set that had worked for me when I was afraid for Chris, and I tried to think that way about my situation now. At Sloan-Kettering, once my brothers left for the airport, I ducked into the ladies' room and pulled myself together, splashing cold water on my face and wiping off the mascara that had run in black rivulets down my cheeks. I walked back out into the street, hailed a taxi, and headed downtown.

Back in the office, I threw myself into work so I could forget my anxiety. I knew we could do nothing more until we got the results, which would take at least another week. My friends knew how close I was to my brothers, and tried to reassure me that one of them would surely be a match. "*Your* brothers, Laura?" my friend Kathy Christensen said to me on the phone. "Of course your brothers will come through for you." I wanted to believe that, but all I could do was hope. This was something no amount of studying or information dug up through research would help me with; it would be sheer luck, serendipity, if one of my brothers was a match. And the role of luck should never be downplayed in medicine.

I also found myself praying, something that didn't come easy to me. My parents, both raised in strict Catholic households, left the church when I was in second grade, after deciding they didn't want to raise us with Catholicism's social prohibitions and its emphasis on guilt and sin. In an effort to find another form of religious instruction for us, my mother joined the Unitarian Church, which we attended for a few years. But my mother's feeling about God, she later explained to us, was in her own heart, an intensely personal feeling. She felt we would have to find our own way as well, and we would be free to chose whatever religion we wanted when we grew up. My father simply called himself a "nonparticipating humanist," which sounded pretty good to me.

Still, I understood the comfort religion provided to believers, and facing death made me think about my own vague idea of God. "Sometimes I try to pray, but after all these years I'm not sure how to, or to whom," I wrote in my journal. "How can I turn to something I haven't previously acknowledged for comfort? Why should God talk to me?" I also believed, as my mother did, that if there was a God, he wasn't someone you could ask to intervene in your personal affairs. But that kind of rational thinking goes out the window when your life is threatened. It's almost instinctive to say, as we did now, "Please, God. . . ." And there were prayers being said for me, too, by more qualified petitioners, from my devout Catholic aunts and uncles to Sister Pearl and Sister Alma, the nuns who worked with my mother.

Four days after the tests on my brothers, with still no word on the results, I had my first taste of what this disease could do to me. I had just finished editing a story for the five-thirty deadline, when my side began to ache more than usual. I tried to ignore it, but I was getting short of breath and a little panicked. I called Dr. Gaynor, who said he would meet me at the emergency room of New York Hospital as soon as he could. My fiancé and I took a cab over, arriving to a scene of near-bedlam, with howling babies, babbling homeless people, and some obviously psychotic cases. After an hour of waiting, I felt I couldn't take it any more. "I want to leave," I said. "I would have to be dying to want to stay at this place another minute."

He persuaded me to stick around, and an intern finally examined me and told me he needed to check my blood gases. I was by now used to needles in the veins of my arms, but I was unprepared for what happened next. The intern took my hand, bent back my wrist, and inserted a long needle into the artery. After an unsuccessful jab at my left wrist, he went after the one in the right wrist.

I nearly fainted as he jiggled the needle around and finally withdrew his sample. Then he piled me onto a wheelchair and I was transported along seemingly endless corridors to a room where my left arm was injected with radioactive isotopes to prepare for a nuclear medicine scan. "GE," I read on the massive metal cylinder that was lowered over me, as the company's slogan ironically popped into my head, "We bring good things to life."

Dr. Gaynor finally arrived to supervise the next steps, a chest X ray and another blood test from my right arm, barely healed since blood had been drawn that morning. Pretty soon they had a result: below-normal blood oxygen, much as if I had been smoking a couple of packs of cigarettes a day. The good news was that I wasn't having a pulmonary embolism as had been suspected, and I wouldn't have to have my spleen surgically removed, as had also been feared.

But my white cell count was climbing, and Dr. Gaynor decided it was time to put me on the drug hydroxyurea, which at least temporarily would stem the flood of white blood cells that my defective marrow was pumping into my bloodstream. The drug doesn't stop the disease, but for a while it effectively slows down the production of abnormal cells. Anyway, it made me feel better, and I was back at work two days later.

On November 15, I went to Dr. Gaynor's office in the morning for a blood test to monitor my white blood cell count and make sure the disease wasn't progressing. I arrived to find that Dr. Gaynor was behind closed doors, and I began to suspect the worst. I felt sure he already knew my brothers weren't a match but wasn't telling me. As the nurse stuck the needle in my arm, I started to cry. "Oh no, don't cry, you are our bravest patient, always so up," she said soothingly. She told me Dr. Gaynor still didn't know anything, but promised he would call me that afternoon with the results of my brothers' tests.

At 6:30 P.M., I was still sitting in my office, and Dr. Gaynor still hadn't called. Resting my chin on my palm, I gazed over at the bulletin board to the left of my desk, crammed with pictures of family, friends, movie sets I had been on, parties I had been to—my fast-receding normal life. Part of the bulletin board looked like a shrine to my brothers, including two portraits of them in their military uniforms, Art in his Air Force blue and Chris in his Marine fatigues.

The phone startled me out of my reflection. It was Dr. Gaynor, apologizing for taking so long to get back to me. "I just wanted to make absolutely sure that the test results were right," he told me. "But I have amazing news—it looks like both your brothers are a match." I almost didn't believe him. Then I started to cry, but this time out of relief and joy. Through my tears I stared over again at the photos of Art and Chris, and it seemed as if their sparkling eyes were looking right into mine, smiling back at me as if to say, "You doubted us?"

Against all odds, the three of us had the exact genetic makeup necessary to qualify us as identical sibling matches, a piece of luck that would give one of them a chance to save my life instead of helplessly standing by. As Dr. Gaynor said good-bye, he added, "I think you have a guardian angel."

Maybe, just maybe, he was right. We were over the biggest hurdle—for now.

THREE

PRESERVING
A CHANCE

Now I had another issue to think about.

One of the most devastating aspects of facing cancer at a relatively young age is that the chemotherapy and radiation treatments designed to save your own life may destroy your ability to have children. There are a number of things that can be done about the issue of infertility, but all involve difficult choices in the midst of an already harrowing situation. It's an area of medicine in which tremendous strides are being made every day, and in October of 1997 scientists announced they have found a way to freeze the eggs of women who are about to undergo chemo or radiation, so that eventually, the eggs can be fertilized with a partner's sperm, and the embryos implanted in the womb.

But in 1991, when I was facing this dilemma, egg freezing wasn't yet an option. Fertility specialists knew how to freeze sperm, and they could freeze an embryo made from an egg that had been fertilized with sperm, but they had not yet figured out how to make an egg survive the cryopreservation process. That meant men could independently preserve the option to have children by freezing sperm, but a woman had to have a partner whose sperm could be used to fertilize her eggs before the resulting embryo could be frozen.

In early November, my fiancé and I sat down with Dr. Gaynor in his office to talk about my options. "Is there any chance I could still have a baby after a bone marrow transplant?" I asked him.

Gaynor was frank. "I'm afraid the chemotherapy and radiation that you get to prepare you for a transplant will leave you infertile," he said. "But some couples who are going through this kind of thing are storing frozen embryos, which is an option you should explore right away."

I was well aware of in vitro fertilization (IVF), as a number of women I knew had been through it. Using fertility drugs, a woman is able to produce multiple eggs, which are then extracted and fertilized in petri dishes with her husband's sperm. The "test tube" embryo is then inserted in her womb. In some cases I knew of, it had produced a pregnancy; in many, it had not. In my case, Gaynor explained, the embryos could be frozen until I was ready to use them, usually up to five years. He had connections to the in vitro clinic at Cornell University's New York Hospital, and though there was a waiting list, he was certain my condition could get me to the top of it right away.

Of course, there were potential risks. I would have to be injected with massive doses of hormones to accelerate the production of eggs, so that instead of the single egg produced in a normal menstrual cycle, there would be several. The hormones themselves might have some effect on my blood counts or my immune system, and they might make me feel even worse than I already did, Gaynor warned.

"What about just trying to get pregnant now?" I asked him.

"Bad idea," he responded. "If your disease takes an unanticipated turn for the worse while you're seven months pregnant, both your life and your baby's life would be in danger."

So my only shot at having a biological child would be to take the hormones, go through the in vitro process, and try to freeze some fertilized embryos. We thanked Gaynor and went home to talk about it. I felt that the risks were ones I was willing to take if the procedure would preserve our ability to have a child together. My fiancé agreed to go along.

A few days later, I was in the office of Dr. Zev Rosenwaks, a handsome, obviously brilliant, and self-assured Israeli-born fertility specialist who was one of the pioneers of in vitro science. Though I wasn't yet married, as required by the center, Dr. Rosenwaks agreed to take me on as a patient, given the urgency of my situation. "Ordinarily we resist this for nonmarried people," he told me. "It's an ethical issue—we're not worried about getting sued." Still, he produced some legal documents for us to sign, which basically said that in the case of divorce, neither could use the embryos without the other's consent. We asked him what happened in the event that we didn't or couldn't use the embryos. "They are destroyed," he told us.

Rosenwaks explained that in standard IVF procedures, several embryos were usually implanted in a woman right after they were created, with about a 30 percent chance that one or more would result in a pregnancy. Depending on how many embryos resulted from an in vitro cycle, there were often some left over, and Cornell's practice was to freeze them for five years. But he warned me that the hospital hadn't yet had a successful pregnancy from frozen embryos, and certainly had never tried to make anyone pregnant after a bone marrow transplant. "I'm ready to be the first," I told him.

The in vitro clinic was a world away from the depressing halls of Sloan-Kettering, but there was another kind of desperation at Cornell: the women there were dying to have children. They were ready to defy all odds of nature and to pay whatever was necessary—and that was plenty. The first thing you had to do was fork over about $7,000, hardly any of it covered by most medical insurance policies. "What a racket," I remember saying to myself as I handed over my money and entered a waiting room packed with women. But sometimes you have to dig into your own pocket for something this important, and the investment, though risky, was worth it to me. My insurance covered only incidental costs, such as blood tests.

For the next month I shuttled between these two very different medical environments—the fertility clinic and the cancer center. On Tuesday, November 18, I was scheduled for a "teaching session" at Cornell. My fiancé was out of town on business so I went alone. In addition to myself, the class included three married couples from very diverse backgrounds: a middle-class teacher and her husband from New Jersey, an investment banker and his lawyer wife, and an anxiously childless Orthodox Jewish pair from Brooklyn. Each morning, the nurse instructed, we women would plunge a small syringe filled with the follicle-stimulating hormone Lupron into our thighs; each evening the men would have to plunge a much longer needle filled with the hormones Pergonal or Metrodin into our backsides.

The nurse demonstrated the technique on an orange. "Think of it as throwing a dart," she told the men, who looked horrified as she casually mentioned that it would be very dangerous to hit a muscle or have an air bubble in the syringe that might cause a blood clot. Worried about how my fiancé would handle the needle he hadn't been instructed to use, I asked one of the nurses in the clinic if I could pay her to give me my evening shot.

So now, every day for the next three weeks I had to wake up at six in the morning, grab a taxi, and get over to Cornell's in vitro clinic at York Avenue and Seventieth Street. There I would get daily blood tests to monitor hormone levels and get ultrasounds of my ovaries to see if egg follicles were developing as hoped. After that, I would go downtown to the office. At night, after dinner, I would jump in another cab and go thirty blocks south and five blocks east to the nurse's house for my shot in the rear end, then turn around and come back home.

I was already trying to juggle my regular doctor appointments with Dr. Gaynor and the team at Sloan-Kettering with my full-time workload. Since I didn't have to be at work before 10 A.M., that gave me two to three hours in the morning that I could utilize. I realized I would have to find the time to do everything that was required. And though I was terrified of needles—especially the idea of sticking one in myself—I had to accept that they were now a daily fact of life. "You can always raise the bar on what you can take, how much you can stand," I wrote in my notebook. "Just raise it. Raise that bar."

The role of men in this in vitro procedure was fairly simple if they didn't have to give the shots. A room with a TV and video recorder, a comfortable chair, and some porno movies was provided along with a small vial in which to catch semen. There were two visits to this room, once for a fertility test, and later, to collect the sperm necessary to fertilize the eggs. You had to giggle at the sight of the husbands all sitting outside this room reading the paper and checking their watches as each waited his turn. Once finished, he would knock on a door down the hall; it would open a crack, emitting an icy blast of air. A shrouded cryopreservation technician with gloves and booties would grab the little tube of semen and slam the door again.

My doctors at Sloan-Kettering agreed that I could put off my bone marrow transplant until late spring or early summer. My fiancé and I set March 7 as our wedding date, and I had decided to go all out, giving a party for 200 guests. Though it added to the burden of things to keep track of, working on the wedding was a welcome antidote to researching leukemia and running around to doctors' offices and the in vitro clinic.

I felt much better thanks to the drug hydroxyurea. At work, I often had three screens active on my computer: a story I was writing or editing, notes on conversations I was having with doctors and researchers about bone marrow transplants, and a file on wedding details. After work I would spend a couple of hours running around New York to look at ballrooms and party spaces, grabbing dinner on the fly.

On Saturday, November 23, my friend Nancy and I made an expedition to Brooklyn, home of the wedding emporium Kleinfeld's, to find me a wedding dress. As we walked into the packed storefront waiting room, I surveyed the hordes of young women in their early twenties. "I feel more like the mother of the bride," I whispered to Nancy.

The cavernous fitting area was in a state of cheerful chaos, with young women in T-shirts and underwear popping in and out of their fitting rooms, yelling for help to their friends and mothers, clutching scraps of paper with dream dresses from bridal magazines. I firmly rejected my saleswoman's first offerings of billowing dresses with yards of silk, lace, and beads, asking her to show me something more tailored and elegant.

Nancy darted around selecting candidates herself, dragging dresses into the fitting room and waving them at me, including a stunning Carolina Herrera number. It seemed perfect, until I looked at the $4,000 price tag. Finally, I found something similar for less than half the price. As I tried on shoes, a veil, and the dozen other things it appeared I had to have before I could walk down the aisle in style, I forgot for a while that I was sick, that my body was pumped full of drugs, that my future was a big question mark. I was just a woman picking out a wedding dress, wanting to look pretty.

Three days later, I headed to Pittsburgh to spend Thanksgiving with my family. My parents hadn't seen me since the diagnosis a month earlier, and this was the first time our family would be together in one place. I also had two dozen relatives who were clamoring to see me. "Now that the initial shock is past tense, gather your forces and proceed to get well!" my uncle Alf, my dad's older brother, had written in a letter urging me to come home for the holiday. "None of us will entertain any thought other than this!"

My brother Art drove down from Connecticut to meet me at the airport for the hour-long flight. As I walked off the plane in Pittsburgh, I instantly spotted my mother's face at the gate, anxious and vulnerable. As she embraced me, I tried to be cool and serene, for her sake as much as mine. Soon after we walked into my parents' house, my brother Chris and my father rushed in from a flurry of preholiday errands, both hugging me for a long time. Their pain, too, was in their faces. "I must be strong for me and them," I wrote later in my diary. "I must get better, back to being the one who can look after them, take care of everyone."

But now I needed them to take care of me. That night, I fell asleep in my parents' bed, listening to the sounds of my father and brothers downstairs laughing and talking and watching an old war movie on TV, their favorite bonding activity. I fell into the deepest sleep, secure if only for a little while in the knowledge that the people I loved most in the world were in the same house with me. I knew that their lives were on hold now, too, much as they had been when Chris was in the Persian Gulf. As it had been then, nothing would really be okay for any of them again until I was safely out of danger.

The next day we piled in the car for the forty-five-minute drive over the river and across the interstate to Brownsville, Pennsylvania, the ancestral home of my father's family. The whole clan was there: aunts, uncles, cousins, assorted in-laws, and young children. There were so many of us that the family had rented out the basement of the local firehall for our Thanksgiving feast. We had to keep the food hot on Bunsen burners, and use Styrofoam plates and cups. We sat at long tables usually used for bingo, under a giant bingo board, but we had a great time, as I always did with my relatives. Before long everyone was laughing, telling jokes, and taking pictures. "You take care of yourself, Laura," my aunt Ginny whispered to me as we left, hugging me hard. "Don't you go wearing yourself out."

Back at my parents' house that night I dreamed about a blond-haired little girl. Maybe it was me as a child, maybe she was my own future child. She was too far away for me to get a close look at her, and kept disappearing around a corner when I tried to run after her. When I awoke, I was crying, wondering if there really ever would be a child, if any of this would work, if I was depending too much on science, fostering unrealistic hopes.

But the next day, I was back on a plane in order to get home in time for my regular appointment at the IVF clinic. My ovaries were working overtime on the megadoses of hormones. As usual, for the next two weeks I would go to the crowded waiting room first thing in the morning, waiting for as long as an hour for my turn for blood tests and ultrasounds. To pass the time, most women read the newspaper or a book, or worked out of their briefcases; one strange lady, with a wig and an English accent, sat knitting every day.

One woman I sat next to warned me, "You really have to look after yourself here; the nurses are nice but busy, the doctors completely distracted." Another woman next to her chimed in that this was her third attempt at IVF; each time she had the same doctor, and yet he never remembered her from one time to the next. A forty-six-year-old former hippie with spiky punk-style gray hair told me she had tied her tubes after several unwanted pregnancies two decades ago. Now she had a younger husband and wanted a baby. It was her third attempt at IVF too. I kept my story to myself. I was the only one whose embryos would be rushed off to the freezers instead of implanted in me for an immediate pregnancy attempt.

Finally, on December 10, it was time to "retrieve" my eggs. The ultrasound indicated the hormones had worked, inducing me to produce multiple eggs. I was taken to a pre-op room and given an anesthesia so the doctors could go in and literally suck them off my ovaries with a special device. The last thing I remember is having my feet put in stirrups. I awoke groggily to hear someone saying the doctors had retrieved ten eggs. That sounded good to me, but they still had to be fertilized or they were useless. After an hour in the recovery room I limped home to wait for news.

The next day, I was so sore I felt as if someone had kicked me in the gut. But it was worth it. The hospital called to say that nine of the eggs had been fertilized and the resulting embryos had been successfully frozen. I didn't know quite what to feel at the news. I didn't want to get too excited, and I was a long way from even thinking about having a child. But still, there it was. In some crystalline form, suspended in time, were nine possible miracles, the first glimmerings of life. Someday one of these embryos could turn into a beautiful infant—my baby.

It was another reason to do whatever I had to do to stay alive.

FOUR

THE T CELL DEBATE

Now it was time to get down to business.
Sloan-Kettering wanted to do more tests to confirm that both my brothers matched, and to determine if one brother would be a better candidate than the other. I was not to see Dr. Golde again; now that I was officially a patient, I was assigned to one of the young doctors on the transplant team. "Normally one only has a one-in-four chance of matching a sibling, so you have certainly beat the odds in this regard," my new doctor told me in a letter. "For now let's assume either brother will be okay, but the final selection will depend on factors such as relative age, exposure history to infectious diseases, and availability for transfusion support after transplant."

As the younger of my two brothers, Chris would have been the first choice to donate marrow, but the doctors were worried about the risks of his Persian Gulf service. Though he had not been exposed to any chemical warfare agents that he knew of, many of the troops had been infected by a hard-to-detect parasite that thrived in the desert. The Pentagon had sent out a directive to hospitals prohibiting Gulf War veterans from giving blood until more specific tests could be designed. In theory, anything Chris had picked up in the desert would be passed along to me with his blood and marrow, so Art was officially designated as my donor.

But something else was starting to worry me. In our research on bone marrow transplants, my fiancé noticed that there was a raging debate about the most effective way to perform the procedure. Marilyn, delving into the medical studies she found through Medline, turned up a number of scientific papers that confirmed that crucial fact: there were two schools of thought on what to do with the donor's marrow before giving it to the leukemia patient—and Sloan-Kettering, my hospital, was pursuing the method that clearly wasn't working as well on patients like me.

To understand it, we had to read up on the history of bone marrow transplants. The technique had been pioneered in the 1960s, when researchers were looking for a way to treat leukemia, a disease once thought incurable. Scientists initially tested their theories on dogs and cats. The first successful human transplant occurred in 1968, and since then, transplants had been used to treat leukemia, aplastic anemia, lymphomas such as Hodgkin's disease, multiple myeloma, and various immune deficiency disorders. More recently, transplants were being used in cases involving solid tumors such as breast cancer and ovarian cancer.

Before a transplant, patients were "conditioned" with near-lethal doses of chemotherapy and total-body irradiation to kill off malfunctioning marrow, destroy the cancerous cells and knock out the immune system temporarily to prevent rejection of the donor marrow. The gravest concern was the possibility of death from this problem we had heard about before, graft-versus-host disease, usually referred to by the acronym GVH.

GVH is basically a fight between the donor marrow and the patient's body. Even in an exact sibling match, the T cells of the donor marrow, recognizing that the patient's tissues are not their own, might attack as they would any foreign body. Usually they go for the skin, the liver, and the gastrointestinal (GI) tract, and can badly damage the organs in the process. I read with morbid curiosity about GVH, picturing the 1970s movie *Fantastic Voyage,* where a miniaturized Racquel Welch gets injected into a human body only to be engulfed by defending killer cells. But it was really the other way around, as if Racquel went in there and attacked all those organs she was exploring.

GVH was a hard concept to grasp. Randy Smith, a friend at work whom I often turned to for his analytical abilities, started calling GVH "houseguest disease," which was one way of looking at it, since houseguests often become the bane of their hosts. But it was hard to reconcile that the donor's marrow that matched your marrow, and could save your life, could also more or less turn on you—and even kill you. There were two kinds of graft-versus-host disease: acute, which usually attacked within three months of the transplant, and chronic, which could show up later and last much longer. GVH sometimes killed the patient quickly or manifested itself by causing severe rashes, jaundice, nausea, abdominal pain, and diarrhea. The chronic form could cause the skin to become hardened, scaly, dry, and discolored. The membranes of the mouth and eyes could also dry up, and the esophagus, liver, and GI tract could be damaged.

During the 1980s, the top bone marrow transplant centers had been worried enough about graft-versus-host disease to try to find ways to avoid it. They figured out that the main cause of graft-versus-host disease was the donor's T cells, the foot soldiers of the immune system. By stripping the T cells out of the donor's marrow before giving the new marrow to the leukemia patient, they decided, the fight between the graft and the host could be eradicated. Sloan-Kettering, it turned out, had been at the forefront of this technique, had won grants to study it, and was determined to prove it could work.

But little by little, other major centers had dropped this approach. Our reading of the literature turned up a number of studies strongly suggesting serious problems could result from T cell removal. For one thing, after the T cells were removed, it was found, the cancer cells more often returned. Taking the T cells out did appear to lessen substantially the risk of GVH, but what was the point if taking the T cells out also made the transplant far less effective in curing the leukemia? Patients were making it through the harrowing transplants free of GVH only to suffer a relapse of the leukemia within a year or two.

Many of the studies of bone marrow transplantation indicated that there was actually some benefit to graft-versus-host disease: if the graft was fighting the host, it also might be fighting off any stray leukemia cells. This was called the graft-versus-leukemia effect. The problem was, in order to get that effect, you only wanted a little graft-versus-host disease. But while there were drugs to control GVH, it was difficult to predict how severe the disease would be, and there was no way to regulate the amount of GVH to make sure you got only a little.

Marilyn produced a pile of papers for us to consider. Most were in jargon I couldn't fully understand. Looking at medical papers can be completely intimidating; it seems as if they are written specifically so that only rocket scientists who have had twelve years of graduate school can decipher them. But after some indoctrination, I found that most papers used plain enough English when it came to discussing the most important findings or the conclusion.

For example, a 1988 paper from the *Annals of Internal Medicine* titled "Bone Marrow Transplantation for Chronic Myelogenous Leukemia in Chronic Phase" bore the subtitle, "Increased Risk for Relapse Associated with T Cell Depletion." Among the 405 patients in the study, "the T cell depleted grafts are associated with an increased probability of relapse," it said. That seemed pretty clear to me.

To be sure, the study showed that the T cell depleted transplants were more effective in fighting off graft-versus-host disease: only 15 percent of the patients who had T cell depleted transplants got moderate to severe GVH, compared with 51 percent of the patients who had conventional transplants. But Marilyn highlighted an alarming statistic in yellow marker: the three-year probability of relapse for 318 recipients of conventional, or non T cell depleted transplants, was only 9 percent, compared with a relapse probability of 48 percent for eighty-seven recipients of T cell depleted marrow.

On December 2, my fiancé, my two brothers, and I sat down to talk about the issue with the doctor overseeing my case at Sloan-Kettering. He looked barely old enough to be out of medical school, though he was an expert in bone marrow transplantation, hematologic malignancies, and rheumatology. And while he was obviously bright and dedicated, he was humorless. There was no getting-to-know-you chitchat, and he seemed rather harried and slightly impatient, even brusque. At our meeting, he was wearing a brace on his forearm and wrist. "Tennis injury?" I asked him. "Harvesting bone marrow," he replied, unsmiling. By then I knew what he was referring to was twisting those big suction needles into people's backs over and over again to extract bone marrow. The sheer effort of doing it had given him tendinitis.

For the next two hours we peppered him with questions about Sloan-Kettering's methods and its results. The research report we found on the hospital's experience with T cell depletion was so complicated that Marilyn had spent hours trying to interpret the results from a chart. In the end she had calculated that of all the patients in the study group undergoing bone marrow transplants, only half were in the "disease-free survival group," and more alarmingly, only 25 percent of the patients older than thirty-two years of age were alive and free of disease. It didn't take a degree in statistics to figure out that the majority of the patients in my age group who had undergone a T cell depleted bone marrow transplant were either dead or had relapsed.

"So what you are saying about all these patients?" I asked the doctor. "It didn't work," he acknowledged. But he hastened to say that most of the relapses were in "an indolent phase." As we pondered that remark, he started talking about a drug called thiotepa which had been added to the regimen to make T cell depleted transplants work better. They hadn't had any relapses in the patients getting the added dose of thiotepa, though he acknowledged they only had nine months of data.

The meeting ended as the doctor rushed off to deal with other patients. Over the next week, Marilyn, my fiancé, and I debated the T cell issue. My doctor, however, clearly wasn't interested in debating; Sloan-Kettering did transplants by taking out the T cells, and that was pretty much that.

As a journalist I was used to calling people who didn't want to talk to me and asking them tough questions they didn't want to answer. But dealing with my doctor at Sloan-Kettering made me realize how easily people could be intimidated by medical experts if they weren't used to that kind of reception. When I called him with more questions a week after my meeting, he got angry that I had told his assistant it was urgent. "Look, to me it is urgent," I told him. "This is my life we're talking about here."

He sighed and impatiently answered the few questions I had, but I found myself writing "I really don't like this guy" in capital letters in the notebook I was using to jot down notes from our conversations. I was by now coming into the hospital once a week for blood tests and when I left, it was usually in tears. "Every time I walk out of there I think I'm going to die," I told my mother on the phone.

One evening, I watched a movie called *The Doctor,* starring William Hurt, about a physician with little empathy for his patients, who is suddenly diagnosed with cancer himself and is forced to see firsthand what it feels like to be on the other side. "Physician, heal thyself," was the message. I thought about sending a copy of the video to my friend at Sloan-Kettering.

I didn't do it, of course, but I also refused to let him intimidate me. Though I am sure that isn't what doctors intend to do, there is a natural tendency among some of them to assume a patient will simply take their word for everything. But as a patient becomes more educated in the particulars of the disease and its care, doctors have little choice but to answer questions. In the end, if you are unsatisfied with your doctor, you have to think seriously about finding another one, which by now I had started to do.

With Christmas approaching, my fiancé decided a trip to Europe would do us good. Though I dreaded the idea of dragging around museums and tourist attractions in the dead of winter, I agreed, and we planned a trip to Amsterdam and Paris. Dr. Gaynor was a little apprehensive; my white count, knocked down for a time by the hydroxyurea to 30,000, had crept up to 54,000. That meant I might be more susceptible to infection. And sure enough, our first morning in Amsterdam I woke up with something I knew from past experience was a urinary tract infection. A nice young woman at the hotel's reception desk put me in touch with a doctor. We spent most of the day taxiing around the city in the pouring rain looking for his office and locating a pharmacy that would fill an antibiotic prescription.

The rain was still torrential when we boarded the train to Paris. I tried to make the best of it. We walked or took the metro all over town, hitting museums and monuments. Christmas Eve, we boarded another train to see some friends in a village near Saint-Étienne. We attended a midnight mass, then spent the night in a chilly, crumbling old château that had been in their family for ages. We had not yet told these friends my news, and I didn't want to spoil the general good cheer of Christmas. We took the train back to Paris Christmas day, but I couldn't wait to get home. The rich French food was making my stomach queasy, Parisians were annoying me, and the constant haze of tobacco smoke everywhere we went only made me feel worse.

Back in New York, it was time to do another bone marrow biopsy to see how my blood cells were behaving themselves. On

January 10, Dr. Gaynor called with the results. "Laura, your disease appears to be progressing," he said. "I looked at the slides for over an hour, and there are definitely some more immature white cells." He explained that this indicated my leukemia might be heading into a more dangerous phase. One of the things virtually everyone seemed to agreed on was that transplants were most likely to succeed during the early chronic phase of CML, usually within one year of diagnosis.

"Dr. Gaynor, I'm putting my wedding invitations in the mail next week—you aren't going to tell me I shouldn't do that, are you?" I asked him.

"Well, I can't guarantee anything, but I still think you'll be okay for spring," he replied, assuring me that I was still "the best possible candidate for a transplant."

Though I was still seeing Gaynor once a week, he was gradually turning over my care to Sloan-Kettering, which meant that soon I would be solely in the hands of the transplant team there and the doctor I was so unhappy with. After giving the matter some hard thought, I called Dr. Golde, and asked him to recommend another doctor on the transplant team. I didn't want my doctor to be my best friend or necessarily even to hold my hand; I just wanted someone communicative and responsive who had time to answer questions. It was a tough but liberating decision: you don't have to stick with a doctor you just don't feel confident about. Golde briefly tried to dissuade me, but when I stuck to my guns, he referred me to Dr. Matthew Carabasi, another member of the transplant team.

I instantly felt better about Dr. Carabasi, whom I found warm and accessible, with a sense of humor, and a real willingness to spend the time to talk about the issues. But though he had a far better bedside manner than his colleague, he wasn't able to make the picture at Sloan-Kettering look any more appealing. At our first meeting my fiancé asked him, "What would you do if it were your wife that needed the transplant?" Dr. Carabasi hemmed and hawed a little, but he said he would still go with removing the T cells, particularly since he believed there was a higher risk of graft-versus-host disease over age thirty.

Carabasi was also excited about thiotepa, a drug in the family of so-called alkylating agents that interferes with the growth of cancer cells and lowers the production of white blood cells. Often used in the treatment of breast cancer and brain tumors, Sloan-Kettering had added thiotepa to the transplant regimen to help make the transplant more effective. Marilyn went back to Medline to check if there were any papers on thiotepa's use in bone marrow transplants, and found only one, from the University of Perugia in Italy. It did not inspire confidence. There were only fourteen patients in the study, which concluded that "it seems reasonable to hope" that using thiotepa would make the relapse rate for T cell depleted transplants "as low as that encountered with unmanipulated marrow."

Golde tried to reassure me that the T cell removal protocol Sloan-Kettering was using was good. "People have a tendency to live through it," he told me in a phone conversation a few days later. "The way to live through all these diseases is to survive." If I relapsed, he added, "There is no law against two transplants—you have a lot of options while you are alive." But we had read earlier that second transplants were far more dangerous and toxic, and believed it.

Golde then warned me to think hard about the risks of graft-versus-host disease. "GVH is no joke," he warned me. "Even if it doesn't kill you, it can leave you very unhappy." But he said it would have to be my choice. "If you feel another kind of transplant somewhere else would be better by a significant margin, then that's a decision you have to make."

Golde was right. For the first time, I began to realize there were no sure answers, that no one could tell me with certainty where to go, what to do, or how things were going to turn out. It wasn't black and white. There were risks no matter what I did, and I had to decide for myself which ones I was willing to take. The best I could do was make the most educated decision possible, and let instinct and my own gut feelings guide me.

Though sometimes specialists in a specific treatment will make a strong recommendation for that course of treatment over another, often they won't. In an era when litigious patients have spurred fear of malpractice suits, doctors may be more hesitant to steer you one way or another if there are several options. When a therapy is still evolving, as bone marrow transplantation was in 1991 and still is today, your physician may not feel he has enough data to recommend more experimental treatments that might prove to be beneficial to you. But a good doctor will always tell you that you have to understand enough about the risks and alternatives in order to make an educated decision.

In my case, I certainly informed myself very well, but I was also being told by my hematologist that there was no real difference in the two radically different kinds of bone marrow transplants. Gaynor declined to make a recommendation either way, saying that based on the overall survival-rate statistics he had seen, it seemed like getting a T cell removal transplant or a transplant with the T cells left in was "six of one, half a dozen of the other."

But I just didn't buy that. Everything I had read so far indicated that the Sloan-Kettering strategy wasn't working as well on my disease, CML, as was what is called a "conventional" transplant: leaving the donor's T cells in and delivering "unmanipulated marrow" to the patient. I decided to delve further into the issue, polling whatever experts I could find on the fast-evolving science.

With the help of Marilyn and my colleague Mike Waldholz, I put together a list of people who I thought would be up to date on the issue and might be willing to talk to me. We took some of the names from medical journal articles Marilyn found on Medline, in-

cluding the broad-based *New England Journal of Medicine* and
more specialized publications such as *Blood* and *Seminars in Hematology* and *Transplantation Proceedings*. (Most of those journals are
now available on the Internet through various medical libraries online. The articles appear in abstract form, and many recent issues in
full text. If not, you can usually order the full text directly by regular mail or fax for a small fee. *NEJM,* for example, charges about
$10 per article.)

It was fairly simple to call directory assistance in the cities where
the doctors whose names appeared on the papers worked, call the
main number at the hospital or university, and get a direct line to
the doctor's office. Once again, the reporter's advice: you can never
tell whether someone will take your phone call unless you try. Today, many of the doctors and scientists at hospitals can be reached
easily through e-mail or by phone. Dozens of major cancer centers—Sloan-Kettering, Fred Hutchinson, M.D. Anderson in Houston, Dana-Farber Cancer Institute in Boston, the University of
Pennsylvania, St. Jude's Children's Research Hospital—have Web
sites. Stanford University's Web site allows you to look up the scientists at the division of oncology, lists their publications, summa-
rizes what they are working on, and gives you their e-mail addresses
and phone numbers.

While most of the people you speak with will be hesitant to give
you any specific diagnosis or recommendation over the phone, or
even on an e-mail system that might be used against them in a malpractice suit, the majority are willing to talk over the various options with you. As I found in my first round of research, scientists
were often surprised to hear from a layperson with leukemia. But
once they knew I had read their papers, they were usually glad to
give me a few minutes on the phone, and some of them were downright gossipy. I learned that bone marrow transplantation was a hot
field, with transplant specialists and even entire transplant teams
being wooed away by rival hospitals as different cities moved to set

up their own transplant centers. Though I had been told earlier that Johns Hopkins in Baltimore had a great transplant unit, I was warned by several scientists to avoid it because its transplant team had just been wooed away to Atlanta's Emory University.

Often, the researchers and doctors I talked to would snipe at rival centers, criticizing their methods, their standards, even the doctors themselves. One prominent chief of hematological oncology belittled an expert in the field whom he had once worked with, saying his methods were too "sloppy and unstructured." It was the kind of thing I had heard as a reporter covering corporate America—competitive sniping, undermining rivals, and self-aggrandizement. But many were frank and remarkably blunt.

For example, one of the people I called was Dr. Robert Gale, who had once headed the transplant program at the University of California at Los Angeles. His work had been the subject of a 1984 book called *Life and Death on Ten West* by Eric Lax, about the transplant ward at UCLA. I found a deep file of articles about him, including one in my own newspaper on April 22, 1991, with the headline "CHERNOBYL HERO PROMOTES SELF, IRKS OTHERS."

Dr. Gale had been catapulted into celebrity when he rushed to the aid of victims of the Chernobyl nuclear accident, treating irradiated workers with bone marrow transplants. He had been a fixture on the nightly news and coauthored a book that was turned into a TV movie. But his research ethics had been questioned more than once, he had been rebuked by the National Institutes of Health, and he had annoyed colleagues with his blatant self-promotion. Ultimately he had been removed from his position as director of the transplant unit.

Still, he had published hundreds of scientific papers and his research skills were still considered formidable. I reached him in his office in Los Angeles, and in the few minutes we spent on the phone, he was blunt and straightforward. "Look, everyone feels strongly that their approach is best, and none of them is correct," he told me. "I tend to favor going to a place that has a lot of experience." As for the T cell debate, he acknowledged, "most of the centers now don't believe it's useful to take out the T cells and the results clearly aren't any better. So the vast majority have decided it's not good and they are abandoning it."

When I pressed him further about Sloan-Kettering's idea of adding the drug thiotepa to make T cell depleted transplants work better, he was pretty emphatic. "Thiotepa!" he boomed over the phone. "I wouldn't have a transplant with thiotepa!"

With my wedding fast approaching, I pushed the tough decisions aside for the moment. On January 18, my friends Bob Millard, Skip Stein, and Martine Trink hosted an engagement party for us. A couple of weeks later, Nancy and another friend, Patti Matson, threw me a bridal shower, inviting forty women bearing gifts of lacy lingerie, luxurious toiletries, and the like. I got swept up in the spirit of things as much for me as for my friends and family.

But privately, the issues were never far from my mind. "I'm writing my thank-you notes and planning my wedding, but I'm a long way from all those carefree young women with a million plans and a bountiful future," I wrote in my journal. "I am full of fear and uncertainty, of an investment in something that might be a terrible risk. I've been told I have a 70 percent chance and a 30 percent chance, I've been told time is on my side and time is short. I've been living my life by the percentages, including my chances of having a baby. But I am completely unprepared to face the event. I'm running myself ragged."

Dr. Gaynor noticed, and expressed his concern. "Laura, you are living your life too much for everyone else," he said gently during one of my office visits. "Take it easy. Your health is the most important thing now."

But I felt that I might succumb to despair if I slowed down. I threw myself into work, and there was plenty of it. On January 22, I was about to leave the office early for once, about 6 P.M., when the phone rang with the news that the president of Time Warner, Nick Nicholas, had just been fired. I sat down at my desk, quickly hammered out a couple of paragraphs for the Dow Jones newswire, made a bunch of calls and tried to write an insightful story. I sent an early version of the story in at seven-thirty, redid it for later editions by 9 P.M., and limped home at ten.

The next day, the editors decided they wanted a big front-page story explaining it all for Monday's paper, so I worked the phones most of Friday evening, spent Saturday reporting and writing, broke for another party in honor of our engagement Saturday night in Westchester, then went back Sunday to finish up the article with two of my reporters, Patrick Reilly and Johnnie Roberts. In the midst of this, another top entertainment executive, Barry Diller, called to announce that he was quitting his job as the head of Twentieth Century-Fox, which meant another big story to report and write for the same edition. I filed that story by 6 P.M. and went home to collapse. Though I knew I couldn't go on like this much longer, it nonetheless gave me an intense feeling of satisfaction that I could still do it at all.

As often as I could find the time, I went to my health club, a giant complex called the Vertical Club, and ran around the track, rode the stationary bike, and lifted weights like a maniac. I still had stamina, but my wrists and ankles hurt, and sometimes after a workout my skin looked translucent, the blue veins clearly visible under my skin. I found myself looking at people around me and darkly wondering if they had anything ticking away within them—like that beautiful blond girl with the leopard print leotard cut down to here, all the guys staring; the plump lady trying to keep up in aerobics; the muscled young men strutting around the weight room.

Sometimes I shared these thoughts with my brothers. Once, talking to Chris in one of our frequent late-night conversations, I mused, "I just wonder if any of them have something wrong with them too?" Chris, who had always preferred real-guy gyms to the preening and posing of the Vertical Club, laughed. "Laura, they *all* have something wrong with them." But that was little comfort.

Throughout February and March, I proceeded as if I still would have my transplant in June at Sloan-Kettering. I continued blocking out the pre-workday mornings for doctors' visits, and the hospital wanted to do anything it could ahead of time to rule out possible complications. For example, I was sent to see Sloan-Kettering's dental team, a couple of earnest fellows who pored over my mouth and told me one of my rear molars would have to come out. Since a botched root canal it had always given me trouble, and they warned of dire mouth infections when my immune system was suppressed for the transplant.

So one morning, I had to have a tooth forcibly extracted for the first time in my life. I arrived at Sloan-Kettering early, and the dentist on duty injected my gums with massive doses of Novocain, until I couldn't feel my face or jaw. Then he held my head in a hammerlock for an hour as he struggled to yank out the offending tooth. I made him stop a half-dozen times so I could catch my breath.

Even without pain, the procedure was torture. Usually, at my own dentist I asked for the nitrous oxide gas, which made the invasiveness of having someone rooting around in your mouth more bearable. They offered no such palliative at Sloan-Kettering, however. When he finally pried the last root out of my jaw, I was left with a gaping space in my gum where the tooth used to be, which took weeks to completely heal.

Next I was sent to see the radiologist to discuss the radiation treatments I was supposed to receive. I sat in the office reading a little brochure on "total-body irradiation," which explained, "a mild skin reaction that looks like a sunburn may occur. It will eventually turn into a tan." Great, I thought, I'm going to be nuked until I glow, but at least I'll have a tan. Then I was ushered in to see a technician who told me I would have to get two small black tattoos in the center of my chest and back to act as markers for the other technicians when it came time to get the radiation treatments.

"Wait a minute, I'm getting married in a few weeks, and my dress has a low neck and a scooped back—where exactly are you going to put these tattoos?" I asked. She tapped her finger in the middle of my chest, then poked me between the shoulder blades. "Oh, no," I said to her, shaking my head emphatically. "I'm not walking down the aisle with any tattoos on my chest. You're going to have to do that some other time."

I explained to her that I wasn't going to be getting my transplant until June, and didn't understand why I should be tattooed so far in advance. Her only reasoning seemed to be that we would get it out of the way so I wouldn't have to worry about it later. This was not a good enough reason for me. I grabbed my things and hightailed it out of there tattoo-less. It was to prove a very prescient decision, for I was even then questioning the necessity of radiation in my treatment.

Finally my wedding day arrived, cold, windy, and rainy. I had planned every detail meticulously, half-thinking of it as a party at which I would get to see everyone I cared about in the world in case I might never see any of them again. The night before I sat up at my dining room table until 1 A.M. working on seating arrangements, wanting to make sure all of my guests sat next to people whom I thought they would be interested in talking to. It was a project to stave off my nervousness, my feeling of unreality, and my fear of what I was getting myself into. It was still hard to believe that I was actually getting married, let alone think about the reasons why.

Less than eighteen hours later, my father was walking me down the aisle between rows of chairs in the ballroom of the Palace Hotel, my hands shaking so much I hardly could hold my heavy bouquet of white freesia and pink lilies. From behind my veil I dimly made out the faces of my friends, family, and colleagues, many of whom already knew how sick I was, and some who would learn that night in quiet whispers from others they spoke to.

I came to a halt in front of the rabbi and minister we had chosen to perform the joint ceremony, combining traditions of my husband's Judaism and my own Christian roots. I had designed the ceremony to include the traditional words, the words I had always associated with the perfect wedding: "To have and to hold, forsaking all others." But I was worried that my voice would betray me when it came to the part about "in sickness and in health."

I knew that the words before that were "for richer and for poorer," and I decided to make a joke of it, hesitating a little, looking over at my new husband, and saying the part about "poorer" skeptically. It worked—most of the people in the room were still laughing at my little performance as I rushed through the "in sickness and in health" part of my lines. I got wry glances from the clergymen, but we had avoided what I dreaded most: anything that would make the wedding ceremony seem maudlin or make people feel sorry for me.

As we said our final vows and my husband stomped on the glass that marks the end of a Jewish wedding ceremony, the room broke into cheers and applause and we hurried back down the aisle to the flash of cameras. Now it was time for a party. The band launched into a rock-and-roll set, and before long everyone was on the dance floor. At a lull in the festivities, I got up to the microphone to toast my guests, saying, "I bet none of you ever thought you would see me standing up here dressed like this . . . and frankly, I never thought I would be here either." I wanted more than anything for everyone to just laugh and remember this occasion as a good time.

The next day we went off on our honeymoon to the Caribbean island of Anguilla, where I did my best to enjoy myself, basking in the sun, snorkeling around staring at the colorful fish, feasting on lobster, and drinking rum punches and piña coladas. I swam my laps every day in the pool, but one day I decided to swim out into the ocean. Much as I love swimming, I had been nervous about deep water and sharks even before the movie *Jaws* made me terrified of both. Now I was doubly afraid that my illness would make me too weak to swim far.

But I waded into the surf anyway, and began swimming toward a wooden platform anchored off the shore, watching the ocean floor drop away beneath me. My heart was pounding, and the first two times I set out, I had to turn back. But every day I swam out again, until it no longer seemed too scary or too hard. Finally, I reached my goal, breathless but happy, hoisting myself up onto the platform and flopping down on my back as the raft rocked gently in the waves, the sun beating down on me. This was part of basic training for the future, I thought. Conquer fear.

The honeymoon over, though, I had to go back to the question on which my life depended: was Sloan-Kettering the right place for me? My friend Marilyn, relying on her own calculations, pushed me to face the issue. She came over one night in early April armed with her papers, her studies, and her calculations. It was clear, she told me, that I had to decide between two scary alternatives. Did I want to take my chances with graft-versus-host disease, and go for a conventional transplant with the T cells left in and less chance of a relapse later? Or did I want the T cells taken out of my brother's marrow before the transplant? That would lessen the risk of early death from graft-versus-host disease, but would give me a much higher risk of relapse down the road.

Marilyn was already strongly of the opinion that T cell removal was not the way to go, but she wanted me to reach that conclusion myself. She mentioned that she had seen a notice on a bulletin board announcing that Richard Champlin, the head of the transplant unit at M. D. Anderson Cancer Center in Houston, would be speaking at Sloan-Kettering as part of a visiting lecturer series. His subject was T cell removal, and he planned to describe the new developments in that field that his institution was working on. "We'll just go listen to what he has to say," she suggested. We agreed to meet on the street in front of the auditorium on the morning of April 10, when he was scheduled to appear.

Though such lectures are typically attended only by faculty and staff, no one was checking identification. Marilyn and I were both wearing trenchcoats, our collars turned up against the wet, windy weather. I felt like an industrial spy as we blended in with the entering crowd. I noticed a few strange glances from members of the Sloan-Kettering transplant team who seemed to recognize me from somewhere but obviously didn't place me in this setting as one of their patients.

I had already seen Champlin's name in many of the papers I read about leukemia and transplantation. He had been one of the original members of Robert Gale's transplant team at UCLA, where he had also worked with Golde. He left UCLA to head the transplant unit at Anderson, one of the biggest and most respected cancer centers in the Southwest. He was visiting Sloan-Kettering to report on his center's results with a hybrid version of conventional and T cell removal transplants. Like Sloan-Kettering, Anderson wanted to reduce the ravages of graft-versus-host disease. He showed some gruesome slides of what GVH can do to a patient. (Freddy Kreuger of *Nightmare on Elm Street* came to mind.) At the same time, he explained, Anderson recognized the importance of T cells in the donor marrow to kill off leukemia cells in the patient. Anderson's new method involved removing some types of T cells from the bone marrow while leaving in others so there would be enough left to fight off stray leukemia cells.

I was shaken as I walked out of the presentation with Marilyn. As we stood outside in the cold spring drizzle, I shuddered at the pictures of GVH-ravaged patients that Dr. Champlin had shown.

"I'm not getting GVH," I hissed to Marilyn. But though she was shaken herself, she understood far better than I did at that point that getting GVH might be a more acceptable risk than the method Sloan-Kettering was using to try and eliminate it. "Why don't you call Dr. Champlin directly," she advised. "Maybe it would be a good idea to go down there and see him yourself."

The next day, I called Dr. Champlin in his office in Houston. "I have CML and I happened to hear your talk at Sloan-Kettering the other day," I told him. "I'm a patient there now, but I would like to come see you for a consultation to determine if Anderson might be a better place for me."

Dr. Champlin, though surprised that I had been sitting in on his lecture, was cordial and responsive, spending forty-five minutes on the phone with me during his lunch hour, apologizing for munching on a sandwich while we talked. "With T cell removal the chances of dying in the transplant are lower from side effects, but more than half the people relapse," he told me. "Only a third are long-term disease-free survivors whereas 60 percent or higher using our method or an unmodified transplant would be surviving."

Dr. Champlin was frank in his assessment of Sloan-Kettering's practice of removing all of the cells in bone marrow transplants for my disease, CML. "They have sort of bucked the national trend, and their institutional bias, or goal, is to try and make T cell depletion work somehow in this disease," he said. "Around the world, they are actually the last place really pursuing T cell depleted transplants for CML in chronic phase when there's an identical sibling donor."

"Well, that's me," I replied.

"If it were me, I wouldn't do it," he said. "I know the people there, they are my friends, and that is why I was there giving the talk. But we have a difference of opinion on that issue, and everyone else in the country does too, because no one else does it that way." Dr. Champlin emphasized that other centers had given up T cell removal, "Because what you gain in preventing graft-versus-host disease, you lose in terms of having more relapses."

"But that graft-versus-host disease is pretty scary-looking," I said. "I saw the guy in your pictures covered with GVH, and you said he died of it two years later. That seems like no way to live. I don't think I could stand to be in that kind of health for whatever time I had left to live."

"Well, that's what I was trying to say in my talk," Champlin replied. Anderson, he explained, after years of work on animals and five years on humans, had figured out a way to do "selective depletion," removing only the "cytotoxic" T cells while leaving behind the "helper" T cells. The helper cells were the ones that could attack any remaining leukemia cells. Dr. Champlin acknowledged the strategy didn't eliminate graft-versus-host disease completely, "but there's a lower incidence and it is much less severe."

Champlin rattled off some statistics: about 20 percent of all transplant patients got GVH, whereas 60 percent were alive and in remission. Some 30 percent traditionally died from problems like infection and pneumonia that resulted from the suppression of the immune system.

"Those statistics are pretty depressing," I said. "Thirty percent might die?"

"Yes, in the first year, through problems related to the transplant," Champlin admitted. "But that is the risk one takes for the hopeful benefit of being cured of the disease. With T cell depletion you reduce the risk of early death, but you lose later because the disease comes back."

Dr. Champlin said that of forty-five patients who had received the partial T cell transplants at Anderson, none who had CML in chronic phase had relapsed, though two of the forty-five had died from GVH complications. "We feel really positive that this is a real step forward toward finding a middle ground, where you have a little GVH that you need to prevent growth of the leukemia cells that survive the transplant," he said.

As for my reluctance to leave New York, he said, "It would be a lot more convenient to stay there, but you only get one opportunity, and realistically, you want to give yourself the best chance." Like other doctors I had spoken to besides Golde, Champlin clearly thought a second transplant was dangerous and undesirable.

"I hear you," I replied. He suggested I come out and tour Anderson, and also suggested having Dr. Gaynor call the new patient referral office, send out my records, and set up an appointment to see him in person.

The following week, my husband and I flew to Houston after connecting through Dallas on a stormy night with multiple delays. We checked into a Marriott Hotel and secured a map to find our way through the massive expanse of Anderson, which looked to be about the size of a small city. Everyone seemed chipper and friendly, with slow Texas drawls but an efficient manner. Dr. Champlin, professorial and relaxed, examined me briefly, talked with us for an hour about the scientific thinking behind his new transplant technique, then led us on a tour of the transplant ward.

Though I knew most hospitals isolated transplant patients to some degree because they had seriously compromised immune systems, I was unprepared for the degree of isolation at Anderson. The transplant unit was on a high floor of one of its buildings, built, I was assured, to withstand the region's frequent tornadoes. The patients I saw were placed in hermetically sealed rooms that looked like prison cells; they even had to push their dirty laundry out through a small trapdoor. They talked to their visitors via telephone behind glass windows.

I was persuaded that Dr. Champlin's methods had promise, but I couldn't get comfortable with what I saw at his hospital. All my reading of medical studies and journals had persuaded me to put

more credence in techniques that had been proved by years of experience. I knew there was never any way to predict how a treatment could work out; the best you could do was rely on how well it
had worked in the past, and on how many long-term survivors
there were.

After thanking Dr. Champlin for his time, I decided to do some
due diligence on Anderson's new bone marrow transplant theories.
Back in New York, I made some calls to researchers I had talked to
in the past, including the cousin of one friend who was a researcher
in the field. I also consulted the sister of a former colleague who
had left Sloan-Kettering's transplant team to join a hospital in the
Midwest.

Both women confirmed my concerns. The researcher, who was
from Texas and familiar with Anderson's work, told me, "The most
aggressive new therapy isn't always strictly the way to go." She said
she would not choose Anderson in my case simply because its protocol had not been tested long enough. The idea of taking some T
cells out while leaving others in was promising, but still "too
murky," she added. It might be a good idea for someone with no
sibling donor, someone who had an unrelated match and a higher
chance of GVH. But with my perfect match, there was less reason
to risk being a guinea pig.

Weighing these concerns, I decided Anderson had been using
its technique for too little time to give me sufficiently comforting
data about its long-term success in curing my particular disease. By
now, however, I had at least stopped fighting the idea that I had to
stick close to home to have a transplant. Throughout my research,
the one name that kept surfacing was the Fred Hutchinson Cancer
Research Center in Seattle. They had more experience in the field
than any other center, having performed more than 10,000 transplants.

Marilyn's meticulous analyses of long-term survival and mortality rates showed they had the best results with curing CML in

chronic phase through transplants. My Texas researcher source called them "the Cadillac of bone marrow transplant centers," describing their procedure as "the most strictly controlled, most rational, and most scientifically based of any in the world."

Although Seattle seemed like the end of the earth to me, it was clear where I had to go next. I called Dr. Gaynor, my hematologist in New York, and asked him to recommend a doctor there. "I'll call Rainer Storb," he said.

FIVE

WESTWARD
BOUND

On Sunday, May 10, my husband and I boarded a TWA flight for the long trip to Seattle. Five hours later, as the pilot announced our approach, I glanced out the window, astonished at my first sight of the snowcapped peak of Mount Rainier, rising majestically out of the landscape to the southwest. I stared until it disappeared from sight as we began our descent. I found it awesome, even mystical, and it gave me a good feeling about Seattle even though I hadn't even gotten off the plane yet.

We rented a car at the airport and drove north on Interstate 5, past a Boeing complex that went on for miles, and into downtown Seattle, a glittering little jewel of a city surrounded by mountains and water. Our hotel, the Sorrento, was in the district known as "Pill Hill" for its sprawl of medical centers and hospitals, including Fred Hutchinson—which everyone called "the Hutch"—and the Swedish Hospital, where additional transplants took place. Connected with the University of Washington, as is the Hutch, the Swedish is one of the primary hospitals in the Northwest, and at the time two full floors were leased to the Hutch for transplant patients. (The transplant ward is being moved to the Hutch's new research and treatment facility a few miles away on Lake Union.)

After a dinner of local king salmon at the Sorrento's dark and cozy Jockey Club restaurant, we turned in early. As I drifted off to sleep, I didn't feel as if I were in a strange environment, thousands of miles away from home, as I had in Houston. Seattle felt navigable to me. I had a good feeling about the next day's appointment.

Early in the morning we walked over to the Hutch's outpatient center. Thanks to Marilyn, I had already reviewed Fred Hutchinson's data on bone marrow transplants, and the hospital's excellent long-term survival rates. I was immediately impressed with the friendly, approachable Dr. Storb, a tall, lean man in his late fifties who looked ten years younger. I later learned his daily workout included dropping into a single scull every night after work and rowing about six miles through Lake Washington, into Lake Union, and back.

His accent still bore the traces of his native Germany, but he had been in Seattle for more than twenty years. A graduate of the University of Freiburg in Germany, a Fulbright scholar, and the recipient of a NATO science fellowship, he was an early student of hematology and diseases such as leukemia and aplastic anemia. From the beginning he had been fascinated by the emerging science of bone marrow transplantation.

He started out in Seattle as one of a group of three young scientists studying under the tutelage of Dr. E. Donnall Thomas, who had begun doing cancer research on bone marrow in the 1950s. In the sixties, Thomas became the first head of the University of Washington's oncology division, where he started his radical yet promising transplant research. Working in near-primitive conditions, Thomas, along with Storb and the rest of the team, C. Dean Buckner and Robert Epstein, began experimenting on dogs with leukemia, intent on determining if replacing diseased bone marrow with healthy marrow could cure the disease.

They irradiated the dogs in an underground lab that had been an old naval radio center. Likewise, the first human patients at the clinic had to be carried down the same stairs for their radiation treatments, which would last two and a half hours. Patients would become violently ill halfway through, and most didn't survive. Storb remembers that they sometimes despaired that their theories about bone marrow transplantation would never work.

In 1975, Thomas's group moved its work under the auspices of the Hutch, which they had helped found with Dr. William B. Hutchinson, who named it for his brother Fred, a major league pitcher and manager who died of lung cancer. The Hutch continued to blaze the trail in transplantation; the center was the first to show that my disease, CML, could be cured with a transplant. Thomas won the Nobel Prize in medicine in 1990 for his pioneering work in bone marrow transplantation, and Storb had been working with him virtually every step of the way. He was married to a fellow scientist, Beverly Torok, an attractive, athletic blonde who had her own lab at the Hutch working on such issues as the regulation of bone marrow and blood formation. Curing cancer was now a family affair.

Storb was a breath of fresh air after some of the scientists I had encountered. He was modest, and seemed to have no particular need for personal aggrandizement. When in 1987 he and colleague C. Dean Buckner won a prize of about $300,000 from a Swiss foundation for their advances in transplantation, Storb put the money not in his own bank account but in a fund he set up to help pay for things the transplantation biology lab needed. He occasionally acted as an expert witness in legal cases, here again depositing his fees in the transplant research fund.

Storb spent two hours patiently answering our questions. He talked frankly about T cell removal, a method that Seattle, like other centers, had tried with the hope of wiping out the more dangerous cases of graft-versus-host disease. But he said he and his colleagues had become alarmed by how many patients relapsed after transplants when the T cells had been removed from the donor's marrow. "We dropped it like a hot potato," he acknowledged. The

Hutch was now using T cell removal only in limited cases, and certainly saw no reason to take out the vital T cells from donor marrow when the donor was a perfect sibling match.

Storb was persuasive in explaining how he and his colleagues had been working on different drug therapies that would prevent rejection of the marrow, and minimize the destructive effects of graft-versus-host disease. He reiterated what we had heard before: "a little graft-versus-host disease can be a good thing" because of its efficacy in fighting off the leukemia. But with new drugs, he said, patients could now avoid the really bad cases of GVH disease that could kill them.

Storb had detailed these findings in a 1986 paper that was widely reported, even in the lay press. After years of trying to prevent GVH with the drug cyclosporine, designed originally to prevent rejection in heart and kidney transplants, Storb's team discovered that adding a second drug, methotrexate, greatly reduced the incidence of graft-versus-host disease. The study showed that adding the methotrexate sharply increased survival rates for at least one and a half years after transplant, from about 55 percent to 80 percent, and that was just as of 1986.

"We haven't seen a really severe case of GVH in a long time," Storb said. He was quick to admit that relapse was still a possibility, even if the chances of relapsing after a transplant at his hospital were less than at Sloan-Kettering. In the event that patients did relapse, he said it was no longer necessary to attempt a dangerous and toxic second transplant. The Hutch and other centers were giving relapsed patients a dose of white blood cells, called leukocytes, from their donor, which seemed to knock the recurrent leukemia right back into remission.

After our meeting, Storb took us over to Swedish Hospital for a personal tour of the transplant ward. Relatively speaking, it looked like a much happier place to be than either M. D. Anderson or Sloan-Kettering. Patients' rooms were spread around a big central nursing station. Those who were having transplants from unrelated donors or who suffered from more advanced cases of the disease were in the more isolated "laminar flow" rooms, covered by plastic sheeting. In those units, hospital staff and family members covered their entire bodies in paper and plastic suits and masks before entering.

For patients like me, receiving less risky transplants from sibling donors, there were open, airy rooms where staffers and family members wore face masks and gloves, but were otherwise unrestricted. Patients hooked up to rolling IV catheters did laps around the halls, putting masks on their own faces whenever they left their rooms. They were all bald or close to it, and many wore baseball caps, scarves, or turbans. One cheerful-looking fellow had painted his head in neon colors. "It's the only time I'll ever get to do this," he told us by way of explanation. I made a mental note to start thinking about a wig and headgear.

Though some of the doors to the rooms were closed, many were open, and I caught glimpses of patients sitting with their families, watching television, playing cards. A bulletin board full of photos caught my eye: "after" snapshots of all the transplant patients, alive and well, waving gaily from their new lives.

What struck me most by way of contrast between the Hutch and Sloan-Kettering was not that the outpatient department was radically more efficient or well organized, but that the staffers and hospital workers at the Hutch seemed far more concerned, caring, and helpful. The New Yorker in me at first reacted with suspicion to these friendly, perky people; I suspected they were all drinking too much of that great Seattle coffee.

But after a while, I realized these people were actually nice, and unlike the surly, ornery hospital workers that seemed to populate my own city, they seemed to genuinely like their work and made an effort to reach out to the frightened patients. Storb told me I could be scheduled for a transplant in July if I wanted to come to the

Hutch. As we shook hands outside the hospital, I was virtually certain I would see him again, soon.

That evening, my husband flew back to New York, and I went on to Los Angeles. On the plane, I wrote enthusiastically in my notebook of my visit to the Hutch. "Seattle: everything clicked. It's not too big and inaccessible and ugly. There's a feeling of success there. Rooms with a view. Not that bubble effect. I saw real hope. Yes, the drugs will be hard. There are more risks up front. Twenty percent don't make it. It scares the shit out of me. But I have to go for it. Go for the cure. Go for the best chance of shaking this thing."

The reason for the side trip to L.A. was twofold. I wanted to make one last trip there to see some of my sources in Hollywood, and I had some interviews set up for stories I planned to do before checking out for a while. But I also planned to visit the UCLA Medical Center at the suggestion of Barry Diller, one of the few people in the entertainment industry with whom I had discussed my illness. I figured it couldn't hurt to talk to the people there, to make sure I had covered all the bases. UCLA had produced Champlin of Anderson, Golde of Sloan-Kettering, and Dr. Gale. They had been one of the first centers to perform bone marrow transplants and I was curious to see their facility.

The following afternoon, I drove the few miles from the Beverly Hills Hotel on Sunset Boulevard to the manicured UCLA campus for a meeting with James Gajewski, the young transplant specialist who headed the department there. We covered all the topics—the risk of graft-versus-host disease, why taking the T cells out of marrow wasn't a good idea for me. Dr. Gajewski told me UCLA was still a bit leery of the combination of the drugs cyclosporine and methotrexate, since methotrexate appeared to exacerbate mucositis, a severe irritation and ulceration of the mouth transplant patients frequently got.

Though I liked Dr. Gajewski, I could see no good reason to

choose UCLA over Seattle. The long-term disease-free survival numbers he was quoting me for CML patients were 50 percent to 60 percent; Seattle's numbers were better, plus Seattle had performed thousands more transplants. Scientists like Golde and Champlin had left UCLA for greener pastures and better jobs, and I had heard through my reporting that budget cuts in California threatened such things as the UCLA transplant program. And when Dr. Gajewski took me up to see the transplant ward at UCLA, I saw a tiny ward with only a few beds. It just didn't inspire confidence, at least not when compared with Seattle.

Thanking Dr. Gajewski for his time, I drove back to my hotel, called Dr. Storb's office, and told him I was ready when the Hutch was. "Why don't you plan to be here in late June?" he suggested.

My decision was made, and I felt very good about it. Back in New York, I called Dr. Carabasi at Sloan-Kettering and informed him I had decided to go to Seattle. He sounded disappointed, but he was gracious and wished me luck. He also said he would be happy to look after me again when I returned, for I would need continued monitoring for at least a year after transplant. I was happy to hear that, and I was glad he would consent to care for me even after I decided to have my transplant elsewhere.

My family began to mobilize. My decision to go to Seattle would mean that all their lives would be uprooted, and their own work lives disrupted. But everyone was on board. My mother practically cheered when I informed her we would be going to Fred Hutchinson, my decision having been reinforced by her colleagues in the Pittsburgh medical community who agreed that it was our best shot. She arranged a three-month unpaid leave of absence from her job at the hospice, starting in July. Chris took some vacation time, planning to be with us for the first two weeks in Seattle, since he was an alternate donor.

Art, meanwhile, got the green light from his company, General

DataComm Inc., to take the six weeks he would need to be my donor and then stick around to provide extra blood support such as platelets if need be. I was a little nervous about Art, wanting to keep pretty close tabs on him until transplant time. He was in the middle of an important deal in Peru, and the Shining Path rebels there were in the midst of a rampant terrorist campaign. I begged him not to go again, but fearless as usual, he told me he could take care of himself. He and Chris did both promise to give up one pastime, skydiving, for the time being. "I don't want to have to scrape your bone marrow off the tarmac somewhere," I told them.

There was one more person who would be part of the Seattle expedition. I met Deborah Rosen in the mid-1980s when she began working in public relations for Paramount Pictures, one of the companies I covered as part of my job at the *Journal*. We had accompanied each other to the Academy Awards three years in a row, and the studio sent her along with me during a ten-day trip to Italy in 1989, when I was reporting a story about Paramount's production of the third *Godfather* movie.

Her job and mine often put us in conflict, as I was always casting a skeptical eye on things she was trying to put a positive spin on. I called her a Pollyanna and she excoriated me for my cynicism. But she had a tremendous heart and was great fun, and over the years we had become friends in spite of our apparent differences. She usually shrugged me off when I reminded her that our jobs made it impossible for us to have a normal friendship.

By the spring of 1991, however, Deborah wasn't working for Paramount anymore. She lost that job as part of a management shakeup at the studio, but the company had offered to pay out the two years remaining on her contract. That gave her the time and money to fulfill a longtime fantasy of moving to Italy. She was learning the language, soaking up the culture, doing some consulting work for filmmakers, and meeting all kinds of people. "Ciao, bella!" was the way she greeted me now every time we spoke.

Ever since I had broken the news of my illness to her, she had been keeping up with me through frequent transcontinental phone calls. When I told her that I had decided to go to Seattle, she stunned me by announcing, "I'm coming back from Italy to go with you." I protested that it wasn't necessary, she should use this precious time to her own advantage, and my mother would be there to take care of me. "I can help her," Deborah replied, adding that her mind was made up, and she was coming. She told me she would meet me in New York the week before it was time to go, and rang off. I realized it was futile to resist her.

As I began the mental preparations to face a transplant, I found another valuable resource: simply talking to others who had been through it. There is a natural community among people who have been through cancer, a community that is separate from all the people who haven't had it. Coworkers and friends put me in touch with a few people they knew who had been through bone marrow transplants, and I found that talking to them was as important as talking to the scientists and doctors and reading the medical studies.

In 1991 there were dozens of support groups for cancer patients and their families around the country, though they largely operated locally through word of mouth and referrals. Doctors sometimes put patients in touch with others willing to share their experiences. In the years since then, support groups have sprung up on the Internet, creating instantaneous links among people looking for guidance and advice.

For example, in my research back then, I came across the *BMT Newsletter,* now called the *Blood and Marrow Transplant Newsletter,* which was printed and mailed to subscribers. Today it is published four times annually and is also available on the Internet, as is the text of a companion book on the various aspects of bone marrow transplants. Both were created by Susan K. Stewart, an Illinois woman who was diagnosed with acute myelogenous leukemia in 1989. As she faced chemotherapy and a transplant, she found herself trying to research her disease and trying to find information that was presented in laymen's terms. "There was nothing in written form I could use," she says. "I went through it blind."

As the executive director of the statewide Citizens Utility Board, a consumer watchdog group that challenged utility rate hikes, she had writing experience, so she began the newsletter, wrote the book, and raised money from transplant centers and corporate sponsors such as pharmaceutical companies to help fund her nonprofit group. One of the services it provides is a patient-to-survivor link, which matches patients about to undergo transplants with survivors who are willing to provide emotional support.

Likewise, Laurel Simmons, a Boston-area woman who had a bone marrow transplant in 1987 at Fred Hutchinson Cancer Center in Seattle created an Internet mailing list called BMT-Talk to act as a forum for connecting patients, survivors, and families. Laurel was just twenty-five when she was diagnosed with CML; she was then facilities manager for the artificial intelligence lab at the Massachusetts Institute of Technology. She had a transplant at Fred Hutchinson in 1987 with marrow donated by her brother, but relapsed a couple of years later.

After keeping her disease in check with interferon, she decided to go against the advice of her doctors in Boston who recommended a second transplant, after the people she trusted at the Hutch strongly counseled her against it. Instead, with the help of leukocyte infusions from her brother, she was able to knock the disease back again. Laurel had to rely on her own research and conversations with doctors to make all these decisions; there was nothing available online to help when she was diagnosed in 1987.

"What was so frustrating to me about this illness is that I finally learned everything there was to know when I didn't need it anymore. I had this vast store of knowledge and I wanted to share it, to help other people," she says. She was working at MIT, an institution where starting an Internet mailing list was as easy as walking down the hall and asking a colleague to help her. In 1994, BMT-Talk went on the Worldwide Web.

"I created this mailing list because I believe people who have had or who will be undergoing transplants, and the people who love them, need all the resources and support they can get," she explains in her own Web site. "There are a growing number of people out there willing to offer support and to share information with people affected by bone marrow transplantation." Laurel is now pursuing a master's in public health at Harvard University; she aims to eventually broaden the concept of the mailing list and use the Internet to help break down the barriers between doctors and patients.

BMT-Talk allows you to subscribe by simply sending an e-mail asking to be put on the electronic mailing list. If you are hesitant about introducing yourself into the group, you can merely read the messages that go back and forth. The daily volume of e-mail can be overwhelming, so you can subscribe to it in digest form, getting one summary daily with all the messages attached. You can also search the archives of past messages to find correspondence about a specific subject you want to talk about, such as graft-versus-host disease, finances, or even dating and sex after a transplant. You can send in inquiries yourself, get responses from anyone who might have something to say, set up a private dialogue with another patient. Many of the messages simply seek or offer moral support, but plenty ask for detailed medical advice and query other survivors about specific drugs, new procedures, and hospitals.

Another e-mail discussion group, Hem-Onc, has about 850 patients, caregivers, doctors, nurses, and social workers who share information about treatment. They aren't going to decide what to do for you, but they can help point you in the right direction, tell you about the alternatives to consider with your doctor, and point you to things like clinical trials.

And other leukemia survivors are using the Web to help fellow patients. Art Flatau of Austin, Texas, and Barbara Lackritz, a leukemia survivor who calls herself GrannyBarb, started out with separate Web sites, then linked them together to provide easy links to dozens of helpful sites, including those for various medical journals. Bob Farmer, a Washington resident who had his transplant at Fred Hutchinson, has his own Web site featuring pictures of him and his kids, photos taken of him in the hospital getting his transplant, and lots of folksy advice as well as links to useful Web sites.

Today there are at least sixty major e-mail discussion groups related to cancer, and live "chat rooms" on services like America Online for people with a specific disease or ailment. But even in the pre-Internet days, I found that fellow sufferers were the ones who answered some of the hardest questions: What will I really look and feel like? How will this affect my relationships? What about your feelings about sexuality?

I spoke to a forty-year-old Southern California woman who'd had a transplant two years ago from one of her brothers. She told me she felt like a leper when she was first diagnosed, that people seemed to avoid her and keep their distance. During the transplant, she had lost her hair, toenails, and fingernails and developed blisters all over her hands and feet. She had sores in her mouth and couldn't even imagine kissing anyone again. "Forget about vanity, or thinking about sex," she warned me. "Thank God I had a patient, great husband, because he used to have to carry me into the bathroom. And it took me almost a year to get back to anything resembling a normal relationship with him."

She had also gone through graft-versus-host disease, and it had left her with arthritislike pains in her joints. She couldn't eat fresh vegetables or fruits for a year after her transplant. Sometimes it took her three hours just to get dressed and organized so she could go out of the house. Her twelve-year-old son was so traumatized by what happened to her that he gained twenty pounds in one year.

But her hair, once brown and thin, had come back shiny black, thick and curly. She set small goals for herself, like walking around her house two times instead of one, and little by little, her life had come back. She warned me that after learning you have cancer, and getting through the treatment, "recovery is the second biggest shock of your life."

"Do whatever works for you, and allow yourself to heal," she counseled. "I hear determination in your voice, and you are going to need that most."

As the day of my departure for Seattle approached, it seemed as if I had a million loose ends to tie up, including provisions for what would happen in the event of my death. This can be the hardest thing to face up to when you are preparing to fight for your life, but it simply has to be done, particularly if you have dependents. You need to take care of things like granting power of attorney, and preparing a living will. These are decisions the hospital can help you with, but you should also discuss things with your own attorney or accountant.

In my case, I consulted my accountant and made out a will that spread my modest assets among my family. I had no children, but I was very close to Latisha Burgos, a young woman from the Bronx whom I met through the Student Sponsorship program, which connects inner-city kids with young professionals who pay their tuition for a private or parochial school and act as mentors. Latisha was still in high school, and I wanted to make sure there would be funds to help pay for her college tuition as well. I put my jewelry and stock certificates in a safety deposit box, and gave my brother Art the key.

But even as I planned for my possible death, I did a few practical things to prepare for the post-transplant world. I had been told to expect that my hair would fall out, and after seeing all the bald patients at the Hutch, I knew it was true. I knew patients covered their heads with hats and scarves, but I wanted to have a wig before I needed it so I wouldn't have to worry about getting one later.

My friend Nancy had the perfect solution: one Sunday afternoon we took a ride to the Orthodox Jewish community in upstate New York where her brother and his wife lived. A young woman there had a thriving business as a "sheitl maker," selling beautiful wigs to the women whose religion required they cover their own hair after marriage. I picked out two brunette wigs. Nancy urged me to try something different, telling me "it's about time you tried a new hairstyle." But I decided it would be better to have both wigs styled and cut to resemble my own hair. I had enough to ponder without worrying about a new look.

On the weekend of June 11, Nancy flew with me to Seattle. Our mission was to find a place where my family could live while I was in the hospital, and where I would stay as an outpatient for a month or more after I was released. Saturday morning, we plowed through a list of apartments provided by the Hutch's housing-information staff. The places we looked at within walking distance of the hospital seemed unsuitable to me. They were small, and many were unfurnished. None had any services or security that I was comfortable with. We asked the folks at the Hutch if they had any other ideas, and they told us about a couple of residence hotels that were more expensive but perhaps more in line with what I was looking for.

Nancy and I dashed off to look at both the Marriott Residence Inn a few miles from the hospital on Lake Union, and another one closer to the Hutch called the Plaza Park Suites. Both offered two-bedroom two-bath suites with kitchen and living room at special monthly rates for Hutch patients and families; though the Marriott was much bigger and its rooms far more commodious, with time growing short I decided to book the Park Suites because of its proximity to the hospital. I put down a deposit, reserving a two-bedroom suite from late-June through October. We headed back to New York with a sense of accomplishment, though I was so exhausted I could barely remember anything about the place I had just picked for my family to live in.

All my ducks were now in a row. I began to say good-bye to my friends, acting as chipper as possible and assuring everyone I would be back before they knew it. My staff at *The Wall Street Journal* had a going away lunch for me at a downtown pub, a raucous affair with roasts, gag gifts, and plenty of beer, the kind of party we usually had to celebrate someone's new job or a promotion. I was thankful that their attitude seemed to be that the boss was going away for a while, so we might as well have a party.

But behind the cheerful facade, many of my friends and colleagues weren't so upbeat. It was reasonable for those that knew the severity of my condition and the dangers of the treatment to wonder if they would ever see me again. Nancy, who had been all crisp efficiency in helping me get organized, could only express her feelings in writing. The night before I was scheduled to leave for Seattle, she dropped off a card with my doorman.

"I really don't know how to say good-bye to you," she wrote. "This is the coward's way out. I know if I said too much I would start bawling. I'm so proud of the way you are dealing with this. . . . I know nothing will happen to you because there are too many people that need you too much to allow anything to go wrong."

She added that she wished she could come with me, but assured me she would be there in an instant if I needed her. Finally, she wrote, "It's time for us to get on with the rest of our lives. I can't do it without you. I love you. Nancy."

I fought back tears. As close as I was to the black hole in front of me, it seemed more unreal than ever. I couldn't make myself think about what might actually happen to me, I could only take things one day at a time. From now on, that was the only way to get on with the next part of my life.

A SWITCH
IN TIME

On June 21, I boarded another flight to Seattle, this time to stay.

As the plane took off from JFK, I peered out the window; we made a big arc over the New York coastline before swinging around and heading west. I stopped myself from the morbid reflection that it might be the last time I ever saw the place. My brother Art, sitting in the seat next to me, squeezed my hand, knowing exactly what was going through my head. "You'll be back," he assured me.

Across the aisle was Deborah, returned from her Italian adventure, and prepared for this new one. Chris was already on a flight to Seattle from Columbus, Ohio, and would meet us at the Seattle-Tacoma airport. We had been told to expect to spend one to two weeks in Seattle prior to admission. During that time I would be an outpatient. There would be a battery of tests and regimens for both patient and donor.

My mother planned to arrive later, when I was actually ready to enter the hospital. We decided my dad would stay back in Pittsburgh to tend to his business and would come when he could. My husband, meanwhile, had a busy caseload, but could occasionally work out of his law firm's Seattle office, so he would be there from time to time. Four close friends—Nancy, Marilyn and Noah, and Amy Dunkin, an editor at *Business Week*—planned to use their vacations to visit me over the summer.

But otherwise everything was being left behind. It was if I were heading to another planet, far away from everyone in my usual world. This concept, once frightening to me, was beginning to look better all the time. Being 3,000 miles away from New York now seemed like the perfect way to go through something like this. I could fly off into the sunset. If all went well, I could return again in a few months as if nothing had ever been amiss.

The flight was endless; halfway across the country, a male passenger appeared to be having a heart attack, so the plane had to make an emergency landing in St. Paul. It was nearly two hours before we were back in the air. We befriended a nine-year-old girl who told us her parents were divorced; she was traveling from Istanbul where her father lived. When she fell asleep, Art gently lifted her, stretched her out over three empty seats and covered her with a blanket. I drifted off to sleep myself, happy in the knowledge that, unlike the little girl, I wasn't alone on this journey.

By the time we arrived in Seattle at 10 P.M., the airport was nearly deserted and Chris had been waiting for hours. In fact, he was the only person in the waiting room. He was sitting in the lotus position listening to his Walkman, pretending to meditate. Finally, we retrieved our luggage, picked up a rental car, and headed to the hotel.

But as we entered the rooms, I realized they were all wrong: small, cramped, with no space for anything. "We can't stay here," I announced. "Mom can't live here. I hate this place." Deborah and my brothers, who were familiar with my tendency to complain about hotel rooms, rolled their eyes. But none of them could really disagree with me on this one. The rooms were tiny and cramped, there was no closet space, and worst of all, the room seemed to be perched on top of the interstate.

Chris stepped out onto the small balcony off the living room. "I don't know, Laura," Chris said, shaking his head as he surveyed the cars whizzing by on the brightly lit highway below, "knowing you, I find it hard to believe you came in here, looked out at this highway here, and said, 'Yep, this is the place!' "

We decided to go talk about it over food somewhere; we were all starving, and the hotel clerk directed us to a dark lounge called 13 Coins. As I munched on a sandwich, the Marriott Residence Inn a few miles away popped into my head. "I remember this other, much better place," I declared. "We have to go there right now and try to change." They all looked at me.

"Laura, it's after midnight," Chris said.

"I don't care, we've got to just go there," I insisted. They looked at one another, then back at me. "Please," I whimpered. This seemed like the most important mission in the world to me at that moment.

A few minutes later, we were back in the car, pulling up to the locked doors of the Marriott, a huge modern white structure with a soaring eight-story inner lobby, an indoor waterfall, trees and plants hanging off the inside balconies. We rang the bell for the night manager, a friendly fellow who seemed surprised to find four people asking to see a two-bedroom suite for a four-month rental at that hour. But after checking his computer, he said he had two suites available, and took us to see them.

One had a large living room, plenty of closets, and a huge terrace overlooking Lake Union. At the special long-term rate for patients and families at Fred Hutchinson, it was about the same price as the place we were in. I handed him my credit card. "I'll take it," I told him. "We'll be here tomorrow by noon." We went back to the other hotel, exhausted. The next morning, I figured I would have to do some fast talking to get us out of the reservation at the Park Plaza, but when I told the manager we needed a larger place, she was perfectly amenable. (Of course, I already had sent all my friends and colleagues a flyer giving the Park Plaza as my address, so Deborah had to return there frequently over the next two months to pick up the mail that arrived there for me.)

Details like where your family is going to live and where you will stay after you get out of the hospital may seem trivial, but they aren't. If everyone has to be uprooted from their homes and their daily routines, finding the right environment will make things so much more bearable.

Of course, it was easy enough for me to pick up and go across the continent; I had no children to worry about, and between my well-traveled brothers and me, we had plenty of frequent flyer miles to help cover the costs of traveling back and forth over the next few months. I had help from my company and the resources to pay for living away from home for the duration of my treatment. My insurance would cover the huge cost of the transplant, about $250,000.

Many other patients traveling hundreds and even thousands of miles to centers like the Hutch or M. D. Anderson face problems with insurance, and don't have the financial flexibility that would allow them to live in a residence hotel. If children are involved, there are tough family decisions. The parents of one two-year-old transplant patient at Fred Hutchinson—a schoolteacher and a homemaker—took their older children out of school for six months because there was no one back home with whom to leave them. They ended up crowded into a cramped apartment near the hospital. Fortunately the Hutch has an excellent program called the Hutch school, which helps children who are patients and their siblings keep up with their coursework.

Even for patients who can afford the sacrifices, the upheaval for families can be wrenching, as they were for one couple I later met. Sindy Fedida had to give up her medical practice in New York temporarily to care for husband Andre, a gastroenterologist practicing in New Jersey, when he had his transplant at the Hutch. They were honest with their sons, four and six, taking them on a tour of the transplant ward and explaining in terms they could understand that Daddy's blood was sick and the hospital was going to fix it. For the first three weeks he was in the hospital, they sent the boys home to stay with neighbors, telling them that Mommy needed to spend all her time taking care of Daddy for a while.

But after that, they decided it would be best if the children were with them. Sindy's mother came along to help, and the Fedidas rented a house with a one-year lease that Sindy was later able to get out of after seven months. Sindy tried to re-create their life back in New York as closely as possible for the boys, but it wasn't easy. At one point during Andre's post-transplant recovery, the house flooded, and he developed a terrible fungal infection.

For another patient I eventually got to know, Louisville stock-broker Bill Tafel, the news that he had CML came just as his wife, Rebecca, a dentist, was eight months pregnant with their third child. Though reluctant to let go of his carefully cultivated clientele, his boss urged him to just worry about taking care of himself, promising that others in the office would look after his accounts. His siblings and parents pitched in to help with the children. But once he found an unrelated match and headed to Seattle for his transplant, the couple decided that it was best if she stayed home with the kids; Bill's mother went with him to be his caregiver in Seattle. His coworkers all got together and donated their frequent flyer miles to help cover the many trips back and forth for his family. But at one point, struggling with an infection and fever doctors couldn't figure out, Tafel feared he might die and never see his family again.

There are plenty of horror stories: people who lost their jobs while undergoing a transplant or caring for a sick family member; a family who had to sell their home to pay the expenses of a child's transplant. But while discrimination against cancer patients and their families remains a serious issue, there are ways to fight back, and resources to help with living expenses.

The Americans with Disabilities Act, for example, offers protection against firings and against discrimination in hiring and promotion. It requires employers to make reasonable accommodations for employees with special needs. Sue Stewart's *Blood and Marrow Transplant Newsletter* offers guidance on using the act. Likewise, the Family Medical Leave Act contains provisions that compel employers to give caregivers time off to care for a sick family member. And many patients are eligible for Social Security disability.

Hospitals like Fred Hutchinson also have competent social work staffs that help provide information on local housing in all price ranges, including where to rent furniture if need be for less than $100 a month. Former patients often leave furniture behind and it's available free through a "Lending Closet" maintained by a local church. Van services help transport families around town. The Hutch school serves kids from kindergarten through twelfth grade. Other hospitals have similar programs. Help is out there for ordinary families and the less affluent, and in times of crisis such as these, no one should be shy about asking for it.

On June 24, accompanied by my brothers and Deborah, we checked in at the Hutch. Our admitting physician was Amelia Langston, a congenial, soft-spoken young staff member who was serving as the attending doctor in the inpatient group that month. I was soon to learn that the Hutch was a democratic institution, in which everyone from the interns to department chiefs like Storb rotated through and shared the patient consultation, admittance, attending and outpatient duties.

Once in the hospital, I would be assigned a primary physician who would examine me every day. It might be a resident or fellow at the University of Washington, or maybe a visiting physician from another city or country. Physician's assistants, specifically trained in looking after bone marrow transplant patients, would monitor me closely, administer medications, and work around the clock with the team of nurses at Swedish Hospital.

At first I worried that under this system I wouldn't see Dr. Storb again, and wondered if I would just be in the hands of whoever was on duty while I was there. But I was soon to learn that under the Hutch system, everyone was involved at all times; my case would be reviewed by the entire staff each week. "It's all very egalitarian—everyone gets thrown in the trenches," Dr. Storb later explained to me. "We think it guarantees treatment that is state of the art," he said, adding that for the top scientists, working in all facets of the hospital "teaches us discipline and humility." That made sense to me. And I needn't have worried about seeing Storb; he was to be a frequent visitor.

Dr. Langston and a nurse, Joan Quinn, went over much of the ground covered with Dr. Storb in our first meeting. But then Dr. Langston startled me by saying that even though there was no "clinical evidence" that my disease was accelerating, my latest blood and marrow tests showed some changes that technically made me classified in "cytogenetic accelerated phase." That meant they would treat me with a more aggressive regimen of chemotherapy drugs and radiation prior to transplant.

I was alarmed at the idea that my disease was accelerating, but I also wanted to talk about the issue of using radiation, something I had started to worry about back at Sloan-Kettering. Bone marrow transplants were the only instances of cancer treatment that required so-called total-body irradiation. Dr. Storb had explained that the amount of radiation a transplant patient gets is about 1,500 centigray, or the equivalent of being close to the epicenter of a nuclear explosion. (Without a bone marrow transplant immediately after, that would be enough to kill you right there.)

Though the radiation was highly effective at killing off cancerous cells that were all over the body, doctors were becoming increasingly alarmed about the aftereffects. Studies showed that patients who had total-body irradiation later had increased risk of problems like liver disease and cataracts. Most alarmingly, they seemed to have a higher chance of developing another form of cancer years later.

I had already read up on this subject by the time I sat down with Dr. Langston. Shortly before we left for Seattle, Marilyn found a number of studies on a new pre-transplant regimen that eliminated the use of radiation in some patients. According to the papers, the Hutch was one of the transplant hospitals which already had good results with this regimen, which involved giving patients a combination of the chemotherapy drugs busulfan and Cytoxan alone.

I told Langston that I had read the studies, and wanted to be put on that protocol rather than be subjected to radiation, even though busulfan was sometimes referred to as "liquid radiation." She explained that they were randomizing patients into that protocol; they hadn't yet had a patient who insisted on being put on the regimen. But I was adamant, and she promised she would take the issue up with the other doctors on the transplant team and get back to me. Once again, I was glad for all the research we had done beforehand, for otherwise I might never have known about the new regimen. It reinforced my belief in keeping on top of scientific developments every step of the way in the treatment of your disease, even when you have the utmost confidence in the doctors.

For the next week, our schedule revolved around daily visits to the outpatient unit. I was given a battery of tests on my heart, kidneys, lungs, and other vital organs; the results would be used as a baseline to monitor how the organs were affected during the transplant procedure. Art had to have preoperative tests because he would be under general anesthesia when it was time to extract his marrow. Because Chris was also a perfect match, he was considered a backup marrow donor and a possible platelet donor, so they did tests on him as well. Art also had to store a few pints of his own blood before surgery, and because of my father's history of clotting problems during minor surgery, we all had to be checked for bleeding times and clotting factors. Every virus that had ever entered our bodies and produced an antibody response had to be identified; they had to see what Art and Chris had that might be a danger to me, and what was inside me that might prove a danger to myself. There were X rays, cardiac EKGs, and even AIDS tests.

We were given a patient reference manual consisting of a big spiral binder full of useful information about the Hutch and everything we needed to know about the transplantation procedure, including a glossary of useful terms. I was glad I had already read so much about the process, rather than seeing this stuff for the first time right before entering the hospital.

But, of course, there were some things I didn't know. The manual told me that before admission to the hospital, I would have a central venous line—known as a Hickman catheter—surgically inserted into the entrance of my heart through a major vein in my chest. I found this alarming, to say the least. The Hickman was a large flexible rubber tube used to administer medications, blood products, and nutritional fluids. It would also be used for drawing blood. And it would be the port of entry for the bone marrow from my brother. The good news is that there wouldn't be any more needles.

I reviewed the steps in the manual. The catheter surgery would be performed in the outpatient surgery ward; within a week after that I would be admitted to the hospital. Depending on the preparative regimen we ultimately decided on for me, over several days I would receive near-lethal doses of chemotherapy and radiation, or just chemotherapy, to destroy the abnormal stem cells and blood cells, effectively wiping my body clean to make way for the new, healthy marrow from my brother. Temporarily I would have no immune system of my own whatsoever.

A few days after the chemotherapy or radiation was finished, my brother's marrow would be surgically removed, or harvested, from the back of his pelvic bones using suction needles. The marrow would then be infused in me through the tubes of the Hickman catheter, administered right in my hospital room, much like a blood transfusion. The next two weeks would be the most dangerous, as I waited for the new marrow to "engraft," or set up housekeeping in my bones. During that time I would be susceptible to all kinds of infection and bleeding. And there was always the chance that my body might reject the marrow outright even though it was a perfect match. Although the manual didn't say so, I knew that would mean certain death.

The hospital staff would bombard me with antibiotics and medications to prevent the new marrow from causing graft-versus-host disease, the complication I already knew so much about.

If all went well, the transplanted marrow would begin to produce a whole new supply of healthy blood cells for me. But I would have to stay in the hospital for weeks, possibly months, while this happened. Meanwhile, the physical effects of the chemotherapy would take hold: I would lose my hair, feel weak and nauseous, and experience other kinds of pain. I tried to imagine what this would be like, but of course there was nothing in my experience to truly prepare me for it.

In between our visits to the outpatient clinic and the Puget Sound Blood Center, my brothers, Deborah, and I went for daily workouts at a local health club, determined to get me in fighting shape when I entered the hospital. I swam sixty laps a day in the pool, and worked out with weights. And the four of us tried to make a little vacation out of whatever hours of freedom we could snatch, taking the ferry across the sound to Bainbridge Island, and wandering around Seattle's ports and public markets.

Though Seattle is often rainy and cloudy, that summer of 1992 brought a drought to the region, marked by brilliantly sunny, cloudless days. Mount Rainier, often invisible on overcast days, on a clear day appeared like a massive apparition in the distance, seeming to float just above the horizon. Depending on where we were in the city, we would come around a bend or make a sharp turn, and suddenly the mountain would be there. I always felt awed by the sight of it. The Indians, I read in a local guidebook, had called the mountain "Tahoma" and thought of it as a god. It was easy to see why.

I wanted to make a pilgrimage to the mountain to see what it looked like up close; I wanted to have one day in the great outdoors before I was confined to my hospital room. Our first Saturday with no tests scheduled, we filled our backpacks with drinks and sandwiches, and set out on the three-hour drive to Mount Rainier National Park. We arrived at the entrance close to noon. As we drove for miles up the road that snaked its way up to the visitor parking lot, we dashed out of the car at half a dozen different vantage points to take pictures of ourselves in front of the mountain. We wanted one from every possible angle.

After parking at the aptly named Paradise ranger station, we set off up a hiking trail. Soon, we were wandering through a field carpeted with fragrant purple, pink, and yellow wildflowers, bordered by giant evergreens towering above mountain streams. The air grew cooler and crisper as we hiked farther up the trail, in sight of the snow at the lowest summit of the mountain. We frolicked like children, taking more pictures and laughing. I tried to imprint every scene, every smell and sight in my memory, pushing back thoughts of needles, hospitals, and confinement.

The next day, Art flew back to Connecticut to wrap up things at his office so he could come back for his six weeks with me in Seattle. Chris had a few more days off, and invited Mike Donovan, one of his buddies from the Marines who was posted as a recruiter in Spokane, to spend a long weekend with us. One afternoon, we went to the local amusement park on the grounds of the old World's Fair.

We came upon the park's most popular ride, a whirling machine

that spun around in a circle then gradually tilted up until posi-
tioned like a Ferris wheel, but all the time turning at roller-coaster
speeds that left the passengers hanging upside down while whirling
at high velocity. Though I had never been one for the scariest rides
at amusement parks, I felt I had to conquer every physical fear I
could manage, just as I had tried to do by swimming out into the
deep ocean on my honeymoon. I begged the other three to go along
on this scary ride, and after protesting a while that it didn't look
like much fun, they agreed. Mike and I crawled into one of the little cars, and soon I was clinging for dear life on to the metal bar that
was all that kept us from plunging out of our compartments and
onto the ground.

Emboldened, I wanted to get everyone on the next ride, a tame
but potentially nauseating concept called the Gravitron. This time
Chris and Mike flat-out refused—it seemed silly to these macho
Marines—but I persuaded Deborah to join me. Inside the machine,
we stood with our backs against a padded cylindrical wall, with
nothing to hold on to but each other. As the machine began spinning dizzily, Deborah's long blond mane began to spread out
around her head like a fan, to the delight of some ten-year-olds
sharing the ride with us. I overcame the slightly queasy sensation as
my body was pinned to the wall by sheer gravitational force. We
staggered out into the sunlight. But that queasy feeling was one I
would soon know well.

The next day, Deborah and I had another mission, this time at
a hair salon in the Four Seasons Hotel. Even though I knew my
hair was going to fall out, I guess I was still having trouble believing it, and kept hoping my case would be different. "So there's absolutely no question my hair will fall out?" I had asked one of the
nurses at the outpatient clinic. "There is absolutely no question,"
she assured me.

Though my hair had never been shorter than shoulder length, in
a moment of daring I asked the stylist to cut it all off into a short

bob. As I watched my long brown locks fall to the floor, Deborah cheered me on, promising it looked fabulous. But it didn't much matter. This hairstyle wasn't destined to last very long. I reasoned that losing my hair would be less traumatic if I had less hair to lose. The next day we waited at the airport to meet my mother; she didn't recognize me at first when she got off the plane.

On July 1, just as we were getting ready for my admission to the hospital, a crisis erupted that put my transplant on hold. A staffer from the Hutch called me at the Marriott and said that the preoperative EKG tests on Art had shown an irregular heartbeat, called an inverted T-wave. "We're concerned about the risk of heart attack for Art under anesthesia," he said. They wanted to talk to me and Chris as soon as possible about using him as a donor instead.

I hung up the phone and told Chris, Deborah, and my mother, who had been hovering anxiously by the phone. The news that something might be wrong with Art now sent us into a tailspin. He was still back in Connecticut; trying to stay calm, we called him at his office. But it turned out that he had already heard the news; a secretary in the Seattle cardiology office that the Hutch was affiliated with had just called him to tell him they needed to use Chris instead. Proving that even in Seattle they could lack sensitivity, she'd said to him, "You have a bad heart," suggesting he get to his own doctor right away. As usual, he was pretty calm about the whole thing, but he had made an appointment for the next day with a heart specialist near his home.

The Hutch staff suggested Art get another EKG right away and fax a copy for comparison. He sent it to me at the Marriott on the afternoon of July 3, just before we were due to go to the clinic to discuss the situation. He included a handwritten note, trying to make light of the situation, which he wasn't taking all that seriously. "Here's my EKG," the fax started. "Gee, just now I'm feeling a little funny, my chest is starting to hurt, wow, I'm having

a . . . ACK . . ." and then the words veered off into a jagged line
that ran off the page.

"Very funny, Art!" I yelled at him after reaching him at his
office. "Listen, tell everyone to relax," he replied. "The cardiologist
says I have a great heart, it's just enlarged from all my running, and
the T-wave thing isn't unusual for an athlete," he said. Art told me
he was sure he could undergo the bone marrow surgery with just a
local anesthetic. "Ask them if that would work," he suggested. I
told him I admired his macho attitude, and while I didn't see how
that was possible since it was major surgery, I promised to ask Dr.
Langston.

None of this made any sense to us; there was no history of heart
disease in the family and Art was a marathon runner in exceptional
physical condition. Plus, Art had had that EKG almost two weeks
ago; he had told us on the phone that he had noticed his EKG
graph looked a little off the charts when he was getting it. Why
were we only hearing about this now? And what did this mean for
Art? Chris, Deborah, and I went up to meet with Langston at the
Hutch that afternoon to try and get some answers. I took my tape
recorder along.

"There is an abnormality on Art's EKG that can be caused by a
lot of different things," she told us when we sat down together in
one of the patient conference rooms. "It's extraordinarily unlikely
that this is going to be anything at all serious, but there are two
things we have to determine about any potential donor—one is
whether they pose any danger to you and two is whether the procedure could conceivably be dangerous to them. All other things being equal we'd like to chose somebody to whom there was
absolutely no risk attached."

"But how come it took so long to know this?" I asked, agitated.
"Art told me yesterday that when he was getting the EKG that he
noticed it looked strange. We're lucky Chris is still here in Seattle.
He's leaving tomorrow. If you're going to do an EKG on him it

would have to be today. Why couldn't we have known this earlier? We've been wasting a lot of time in my view."

"I agree," Dr. Langston said. "But I was just shown the EKG for the first time yesterday." Clearly, there had been a communication breakdown between the folks who did the EKG, the cardiologist, and the transplant team. But Dr. Langston was eager to set things back on course. "Let's not waste any more time. We'll get Chris worked up as expeditiously as possible, get all the tests done, and do an EKG on him. Then we'll go from there."

I still didn't understand something: eight months ago they hadn't wanted to use Chris because of the possibility he might have been exposed to something in the Persian Gulf. What had changed? Time, for one thing. Dr. Langston replied that there were no problems in the most recent blood test they had done on Chris—and even though earlier blood tests done at Sloan-Kettering indicated he had a hepatitis virus antibody response, suggesting a possible danger to me, there was no trace of it in the Hutch's own tests. That was a relief to Chris, who had been stunned to hear he had been exposed to the disease—he had never had it as far as he knew.

Once again, we were reminded of how fallible medicine could be. Tests are not always reliable: they can turn up false positives, or they can show up negative when in fact there is a problem. For all the scientific expertise hospitals and laboratories have, snafus can cause labs to misread tests or even miss factors that are crucial to your diagnosis. You can ask that tests be repeated, and make sure that more than one expert looks at them, but sometimes, as in every aspect of life, mistakes are made that can skew everything. Staying on top of things yourself adds one more check and balance to the system.

I pressed Langston on the issue of whether using Chris as a donor was safe. "So if we use Chris, no little bitty parasites are going to pop up?" I asked. "You know, when Chris was in Saudi Arabia I remember him talking about getting bitten by things in the desert . . ."

Chris chimed in, "I slept with couple of camel spiders, but other than that . . ."

Dr. Langston smiled. "Obviously we have to do all the other tests on Chris." As for the hepatitis issue, she said, "We do the most sophisticated hepatitis test available, and there is no evidence that you have now, or you have ever had hepatitis. There are certainly false positives, and I don't know what they were doing there, but the test we have is really quite reliable. And especially since you're not aware of any previous hepatitis, and you don't have any risks for getting that kind of hepatitis, I think it was a mistake."

I asked Dr. Langston next about Art's idea of going through the bone marrow donor surgery with just a local anesthetic such as a spinal injection. She shook her head. "It's the same risk—in fact the risk with a spinal could be higher—and if you do have heart disease, there may be even a little bit more risk because your heart rate varies more." She hastened to add that she didn't think Art had heart disease. "I'm not sure anything's wrong with his heart at all. It may be just a normal variant."

It was sheer serendipity—a luxury really—that I had two brothers who were a match and that one could substitute for the other like this. Most people in my situation were lucky to have one sibling match; if that person was unable to undergo the surgery needed to extract marrow, they might have to go try to find an unrelated donor through the national registry of donors, and we already knew how tough those odds were.

I pressed Langston: "But what if Art was my only available donor?"

She replied that because of Art's general good health, it is possible they would find a way to use him. "If he were your only donor then we would work him up with a cardiologist, and we would assess his risk, and we would all sit in a room and, you know, we would figure out what to do," she said. "There are stress tests, things we could do to establish what the cause of the abnormality is. But we have Chris, so why take any risk?"

I had to agree with her, though I was still worried. I pointed out that Chris was very athletic, too. "How do we know he doesn't have the same problem as Art?" I asked.

"We'll have to cross that bridge when we come to it," Langston replied. "Let's not create problems we haven't seen."

"She's good at that," Chris pointed out. I made a face at him, but I had to laugh. Maybe I was getting a little too paranoid.

"Let's just try and get the tests done today, try to look at them and nail things down before Chris leaves town," Dr. Langston told us. "Art's being seen by a cardiologist. He's probably going to turn out fine, a normal healthy young guy who has a variant EKG and that is all."

I asked her another question. "Are there going to be any more surprises?" Her answer provided yet another reminder that tests weren't always exactly reliable. But I was about to realize that in some cases, that can be a good thing.

"There actually is one more surprise—but it's a good one," Langston replied. "You mean I don't have this disease after all?" I ventured, prompting Chris to interject, "But since you're scheduled, you're getting a transplant anyway." We all laughed some more, but Dr. Langston really did have some interesting news.

"We've looked at the latest slides of your bone marrow and it looks exactly the same as it did at the time it was diagnosed, so you are back in chronic phase by our definition." That meant that in the little more than a week since we first talked, my tests had changed again! I was beginning to wonder how reliable any of these tests were. Langston admitted they were not quite sure what had happened. The only sure thing that could have made my disease appear to decelerate rather than accelerate was the drug interferon, and I certainly had not been taking that.

I pondered this. "Maybe it's all going backward and I'll be fine in a couple of months."

Dr. Langston admitted that the team hadn't figured out quite how to classify me because this seeming improvement was "extraordinarily peculiar." Yes, sometimes tests could show different things; one never knew what a specific sample of blood or bone marrow might show. Because there had been at least one test that showed the disease was accelerating, Langston explained, her gut feeling was to err on the more conservative side. That meant treating me with a more aggressive regimen of chemotherapy and radiation before transplant.

"But won't that regimen be more toxic for me?" I asked her. She admitted that it would. "What if I don't want to do it?" I pressed her. "Do I have any choice in this matter?" She replied that I didn't have any choice in how they classified my disease. "Well, but if I'm in this relatively good phase and in fairly good health, why give me something that would be more toxic?" I persisted.

Dr. Langston replied that because they had seen at least one test that indicated the possibility that my disease was progressing, it would be more prudent to risk the toxicity for the benefit of a more powerful efficacy in eradicating cancerous cells. She said that Seattle's experience showed that if people had advanced beyond the chronic phase in my disease they had a much higher chance of relapse—50 percent or more—if they didn't have a more aggressive blitz of chemo and radiation ahead of time.

"If we know that relapse is your biggest risk and not toxicity [from chemotherapy and radiation], then we are going to give you the thing we know is a lot more effective," she explained. "That's what I mean by erring on the conservative side. I'm not trying to err on the side of hurting you more, I'm trying to err on the side of trying to reduce whatever we think is the biggest risk for you. And if you are in fact beyond chronic phase, then the biggest risk for you is relapse."

I thought about this. "Well the main reason I came out here was to decrease my risk of relapse based on the way Sloan-Kettering was doing things, knowing of course there are no guarantees," I told her.

"There is no guaranteed answer; it's not a decision any one person could make, so I'm going to present the situation to the team," she said. But finally, she agreed on a compromise: to recommend that I be classified as a second chronic phase patient. That was one notch more serious than first chronic phase, which was what I had been in when I was diagnosed initially, but one category less serious than the more accelerated phase in which the one test had placed me.

The good news in all this was that the classification put me in the group of patients who were being considered for the regimen I wanted: eliminating total-body irradiation and instead using a combination of strong chemotherapy drugs prior to transplant.

I had one last question: if they did use the two chemo drugs instead of a combination of chemo and radiation, would that increase my risk of dying during the transplant? Dr. Langston reassured me that the risk of dying during a transplant was about equal with both regimens.

And because I was in otherwise good condition, she assured me, my overall chances were better than someone whose physical health was not as good. "There aren't any red flags hanging out there about you," she said. "And that's very unusual." Langston explained that many patients with my disease were much sicker and also had other problems, such as trouble with their liver or their lungs.

Langston also answered some of my other questions. The risk of graft-versus-host disease was about the same, she said, whether I was treated with radiation and chemotherapy in combination or with chemotherapy alone. There was a slightly higher risk of jaundice and a liver problem called veno-occlusive disease with the stronger chemo drugs and no radiation. But she assured me that while there might be longer-term complications no matter which pre-transplant regimen I used, "you aren't more likely to be a chronically ill person."

I was, in fact, better off than I had realized. My good physical condition would provide the strength I needed to withstand the onslaught of lethal chemicals needed to cure me. At thirty-seven, I was still in a good age group for going through the procedure. I was asking all the right questions, taking all the right precautions, and I felt I was at the right place. Now it was just a matter of going for it.

I knew most of the statistics cold by now. The success of bone marrow transplantation varies widely depending on what type of disease you have, what stage that disease is in, and how old you are. When I arrived at Fred Hutchinson, overall long-term disease-free survival was about 70 percent; for my specific disease, CML, and for transplants done within a year of diagnosis, it was as high as 80 percent. Today, with advances in pre-transplant chemotherapy and other aspects of post-transplant care, the Hutch is approaching survival rates as high as 90 percent.

In 1992, as I prepared to undergo my transplant there, I was looking at a 30 percent chance of getting acute graft-versus-host disease and a 30 percent chance of getting the chronic form. For me, there was a relatively low chance of dying immediately after the transplant from graft failure or outright rejection because my brother was a match; but there was still about a 1 percent chance it could happen. In general, there was a 3 percent to 10 percent chance of dying fairly soon after transplant, and that is still about 5 percent today.

My chances of getting veno-occlusive disease, a severe and potentially fatal liver complication, were only about 5 percent. But I had a much higher chance of dying from pneumonia because I tested positive for something called cytomegalovirus. Many people are CMV-positive; it means you carry the virus and have an immune response against it. The danger during transplant is that while your immune system is knocked down, the CMV virus is still there, and you don't have any way to fight it. If you are CMV-positive and you donor is CMV-negative, you have about a 30 percent chance that you will get the potentially fatal pneumonia; if you are CMV-negative but your donor is CMV-positive, the risk is about 20 percent.

With the news that Chris would now be my donor, everyone scrambled to change plans. Chris had to go back to Ohio to tell his company that he would have to be my donor. I was a little worried about the response, since he was a fairly new employee. He told me to stop worrying as he left for the airport the next day. "I'll be back before you know it and I'll be here as long as I have to be," he told me.

To my relief, Art called that afternoon to tell me his cardiologist had told him he was in perfectly good health after all, but that a very conservative anesthesiologist could justifiably be hesitant to put him under anesthesia for hours if it wasn't absolutely necessary. There was, indeed, a slight risk of a heart attack with his T-wave patterns. "I'm sorry, Laura. I feel as if I've let you down somehow," Art told me. I wanted nothing more than for him *not* to feel that way, so I tried to make him laugh. "Don't be ridiculous," I said. "I don't want to have to live with the guilt if you croak on the operating table just so I can get your bone marrow."

It was only then that I remembered what Art had said to me so many months ago that night in New York, when he predicted that Chris would be the one to "come through" for me. His premonition had turned out right.

It was up to Chris now.

SEVEN

THE INVASION OF
THE BODY SNATCHERS

The invasion of my body was about to begin.

On July 7, I left the Marriott early in the morning with my mother, driving over to the hospital to have the Hickman catheter installed in my body. As I lay on the operating table, the masked surgeon explained that he would make two small incisions just below my collarbone and on my chest wall, enter through the lower incision, and make a tunnel to the upper one.

The catheter tubing would then be inserted in the lower incision, pulled through the tunnel, and inserted into a large vein near my neck. A small Dacron cuff would hold the catheter in place, and would also serve as the barrier to prevent bacteria from traveling up the catheter into my bloodstream. The top incision would also be stitched to help anchor the catheter. But the lower incision's stitches would be taken out in a few days, and the tubing would protrude right out of that opening in my body.

I found it hard to picture all this. The main thing that worried me was the incision he kept talking about on my chest. "But you aren't going to cut through my breast, are you?" I said anxiously as the anesthesiologist stuck the needle into a vein in my hand. The last thing I heard as I faded into unconsciousness was the surgeon telling me not to worry about it.

Three hours later I awoke groggily to see my mother peering anxiously over me. I pushed myself up on my elbows and looked down in dismay at the large white bandage covering half my chest. Emerging from underneath it was the large tube of the catheter, branching off into two smaller tubes sealed off by plastic caps. Though it was painful to the touch, I traced the tube under the bandage with my fingers, horrified to feel that it was indeed coming out of the soft tissue of my breast. "Oh, Mom, look what they did!" I cried.

Though the surgeon was long gone, the nurses and physician's assistants were sympathetic and apologetic, explaining that it was never an exact science where the tube would come out. The idea was to bring it out of the chest wall, they explained, but in my case there wasn't as much flat space on the chest wall. It was the downside of being a 34D. I tried not to think about it, but every time I looked down at the bandage, I felt disfigured. And I was starting to realize how little control I would have over my own body from now on.

The catheter site would have to be cleaned and the dressing changed daily, the tubes flushed with a special solution to prevent a blood clot from forming. To inject the solution, you had to plunge a syringe filled with stuff into one of the two injection caps; that was how everything would be inserted or removed from those tubes. There were dire warnings about the danger of infection through the catheter; after all, this was an open passage right into my heart and my bloodstream.

My mother took care of the dressing from the start. As a nurse she was trained in this kind of thing, so it was pretty standard stuff for her. But the patient manual had a whole chapter on how to care for the catheter for those who were less proficient. Each day, the bandage had to be removed, the skin around the exit site checked for redness or signs of infection, then swabbed with sterile applica-

tors dipped in hydrogen peroxide. Next, the site had to be painted
with a Betadine swab to cover the area with the medicinal-smelling,
rust-colored iodine solution. Then a dab of iodine ointment had to
be applied to the site, and a sterile dressing attached, covered by a
plastic "shield" device.

All this took about twenty minutes if you were good at it, a lot
longer if you weren't. There was a huge amount of paraphernalia
required, everything sealed in individual sterile packages. My
mother had to hold the tube upright and tug at it a little to do all
this, which made me shudder. I would turn my head away, unable
to look at it. Finally, she would coil the tube around the site and
tape it to my dressing. A silver clamp known as a "bulldog" was attached to part of the catheter, which you were supposed to attach
to your clothing. I attached mine to the gold chain I always wore
around my neck, so the clamp looked like a little pendant with the
catheter hanging from it.

I tried not to think about how vulnerable that hole in my chest
made me feel; when the nurses drew blood, they would simply stick
a needle in one of the two caps and release the clamp that kept it
shut. Without that clamp, I envisioned my blood pouring out uncontrollably. I tried to look on the bright side. With the catheter in
place, I wouldn't have to have another needle jabbed into my veins
for a very long time. That would be one less form of torture for now.

That afternoon Chris called; his boss had cleared the way for
him to take a leave from work, and his medical insurance would
cover his own hospitalization as my donor. He would be back in
Seattle in four days. Dr. Langston had informed me that a bed
would be available July 12, the day after Chris planned to arrive.
That was fine with me; I didn't plan to walk into that hospital and
let them start destroying my immune system unless he was safely in
town and I had laid eyes on him. Once they began the massive
doses of chemotherapy, there was no going back and no way to factor in delays.

My husband and Marilyn, who wanted to be there when I checked into the hospital, flew in on July 11, and we all decided to go out for a sort of "Last Supper" before the big day. Truth was, I was still in something of a state of denial. I was trying not to think too much about what was going to happen to me until it actually started. We piled into a couple of cars for the short drive to Palomino, a restaurant specializing in Northwestern cuisine in downtown Seattle. I insisted on driving our rented Taurus, even though I was still in pain from the surgery to insert the Hickman catheter and the catheter itself was just tucked under my shirt. We had to drive several levels down in the underground parking garage of the building in which the restaurant was located, and I steered the car down the spiral entry ramp and navigated it into a parking spot.

But obviously I wasn't as clearheaded as I thought. After everyone was out of the car and heading toward the elevator, I set the lock on the car door and slammed it—with the keys still inside and the motor running. When I realized what I had done, I literally flipped out, screaming at myself for being a complete idiot, crying, and generally losing it. Marilyn, Deborah, and my mother went off to find a parking attendant to see if he knew of a nearby mechanic or had some ideas on how to open the car. Frantic, and determined to deal with this myself, I took the elevator up to the restaurant to call Hertz. Things weren't as dire as they seemed; the representative said he would be able to send someone from the downtown office with a new key within an hour or so.

Inside Palomino, we sat down at a big round table, while everyone tried to calm me down, urging me to relax and enjoy the meal. The Hertz guy came, the car was turned off, and everything was resolved. Still, I was so upset I was practically beating myself over the head. "I'm a stupid careless ditz!" I yelled. But my hysteria over this little mistake, this easily dealt with blunder, was not unlike my hysteria that day in New York when my brothers were being tested and I got upset that they might miss a plane. This time, I was also venting the fear and anger that I had denied to everyone, including myself. I hadn't cried, screamed, or yelled about what was really upsetting me, but obviously I wasn't that good at controlling my emotions. They were going to sneak out somehow.

It's hardly surprising that sorting out your emotions is difficult when you are about to undergo a life-threatening medical procedure that is also your only hope for survival. After my initial terror when I learned I had leukemia, I had decided to try and tough it out. I think I was afraid that once I let go, once I gave in to my emotions, I would lose my courage and maybe even my mind. I had convinced myself that toughness was the only way to get through it.

I had never been interested in seeking psychological help, though I appreciated what therapy had done for many of my friends. Back in New York, when I first began seeing Dr. Carabasi, he had suggested that I see a psychiatrist who counseled cancer patients. But meeting with her just once, I felt as if I was a stronger person than she, and doubted there would be any benefit to continuing the therapy. Perhaps had I given it more of a chance I might have learned something helpful. In fact, hospitals and transplant centers are used to helping people cope with these emotions, and are constantly trying to develop strategies to ease the trauma. Even if you've never felt the need for it before, this might be the time to try professional help.

My friend Marilyn was only too aware that I was suppressing my true fears and emotions. The next day, we went to breakfast alone together at Duke's, across the street from the Marriott, before she was due to fly back to New York. I still felt awkward about my behavior the night before, but I tried to thank her for all she had done for me. This brilliant person had devoted months of her time to helping me do the research that had led me to this point, and I didn't know how I could ever repay her. We sat outside in the bright morning sunlight on the restaurant's waterfront deck, sipping coffee.

But it wasn't until she was on the plane home that afternoon that Marilyn was able to articulate her own feelings. In a six-page letter, she told me she knew that the incident with the car keys was about something else altogether, and she wanted me to face up to what it was:

"By the time you get this, it will all have begun," she wrote. "I was grateful for the time alone with you this morning, even though we were both hiding behind our dark glasses and even though there seemed to be a massive roadblock between my heart and my throat. I've been thinking a lot about the 'key' events on Friday and your questions about them. . . . Obviously you're aware of deflecting emotions attached to your illness onto other less important situations in which you find yourself.

"I saw a very specific meaning in the car incident and your distress over it. . . . The humming car engine was a metaphor for all of the powerful emotions—fear, loss, rage—which are an inevitable consequence of what you are going through now. And I saw the locking of the key inside as a symbolic locking away of those feelings, an effort to put them in a place where you could not get to them, nor they to you. Again and again you said, 'I can't believe I did this. I've never done anything like this. This is the stupidest thing I've ever done.' I thought you were talking about getting leukemia.

"The catheter session on Friday forced you to confront the first of the multiple violations of your bodily integrity and in a very fundamental sense, of your privacy, that these procedures entail. I saw the horror on your face, saw it and felt it. I think that is what you locked in the car a few hours later."

Marilyn wrote that she had learned something important in her own life—that emotions locked inside "inevitably come to the surface." She knew I had tackled my disease like a project, and that I had arrived in Seattle determined to bluster my way through anything that came at me. But, she warned me, "It's high tide now emotionally, both for you and those around you . . . it's important to leave some time and space to attend to your emotions, however painful, to try to get as accurate a fix on them as possible and to express them, at least to yourself if not to others . . . to try to walk through your feelings rather than around them and to get some help with that if you need to."

As for the feelings of my family and the close friends who were going through everything with me, Marilyn sensed something I hadn't had time to notice: that there was some tension, even jealousy among them. ". . . Each of us wants to take care of you and go through this with you, sometimes even for you. All of us are relieved that there is someone there to lighten your mom's load and each of us is envious that it is someone other than ourselves. Perhaps it will be easier for you to live with these tensions and rivalries if you understand that they arise from the wishes of each of us to be with you, take care of you, protect you."

Marilyn's words finally helped me realize something, the importance of which can't be overstated: while staying in control intellectually is crucial to taking charge of your own care, you can't bury fears and emotions. I had focused on finding my own strength and conquering my own fear, on being strong so my family wouldn't fall apart worrying about how I was dealing with things. I had wanted to show the world that I was, in fact, invincible. Those are good feelings to have, and they do help you mentally to prepare for the complete unknown. But she was right; it was okay to be scared, and very important to express it outright when I needed to.

For patients who have been activists in their own health care, as I was, it is easy enough not to think about how you feel. Bill Tafel says he was too busy going on the stump for bone marrow donors and trying to increase awareness of the need for donors in the national registry to think much about fear and his own emotions. "I was going 110 miles an hour, saying damn the torpedoes," he says. "I couldn't stop to be scared. My own sense of immortality, that this couldn't really happen to me, helped in that respect."

But once you enter the hospital, it is hard to avoid your emotions, which may change to anger and frustration. Sue Stewart, founder of the *BMT Newsletter* and the companion handbook on transplants, writes, "Patients who are used to being in charge, taking care of themselves or being the person on whom others depend will find this physical debilitation very hard to cope with." Stewart warns that patients may direct their anger over loss of control at doctors, medical personnel, or even their family caregivers. She recommends that family members treat the patient with respect and acknowledge his or her intelligence. She also stresses the importance of respecting a patient's modesty and privacy.

I was soon to learn firsthand in what short supply both those commodities would be.

On Monday morning, July 14, it was time. I packed my bags with all the things I would need and want in the hospital—some real clothes such as cotton leggings and big shirts to wear during the day, some nice-smelling lotions and shower gels, books, a compact disk player with a pile of CDs, video recorder, and movies to watch. I also brought my portable computer, determined to log into the office every day to keep up with all the stories my reporters were filing. I even had the idea that I might edit some stories long distance.

My mother was toting her camera—in my family, the philosophy was that if you didn't take a picture of it, it didn't happen—and she was determined to record this process for posterity. She snapped the first picture, catching me wheeling a luggage cart piled high with my stuff as if I were on my way into a hotel.

I checked into the tenth floor, one of the two transplant floors managed by the Hutch at Swedish Hospital. It was the first place there had been a bed available; it also happened to be the pediatric transplant ward. After me, the next oldest patient was about sixteen, the youngest was just a few months old. As we walked down the corridor we could hear babies crying and see young parents anxiously pacing around their rooms while little brothers and sisters raced around on tricycles and pulled each other in little red wagons. It was like a strange playground, a mix of the carefree laughter of healthy children, the cries of sick ones, and the quiet, intense conversations of mothers and fathers as they talked to the doctors and nurses about a child's prognosis.

We were shown to a small room right off the nurses' station, which, to our delight, had a great view of Mount Rainier. However, we were soon to realize that its location made it about the worst room on the floor. There was some activity at the nurses' station at all hours, which gave it the feeling of Grand Central Station. In a case like this, I would always advise trying to improve your situation, particularly if you are going to be there for a while.

For once, however, I wasn't the one to ask for a new room; my mother took one of the nurses aside and asked if we could change to something bigger and quieter. There wasn't anything available just then, but the nurse assured my mother she would keep us in mind if something did open up. My mom had an eye on a big corner room where, we learned, opera singer Jose Carreras had had a successful transplant. He was back on the Three Tenors concert circuit with Placido Domingo and Luciano Pavarotti, so that seemed like good karma.

As we arranged my clothes and paraphernalia in the room, Norman Finance and Kathy Schiffman, the two physician's assistants who would be caring for me, came in to introduce themselves. Norm was tall, bespectacled, and good-natured; Kathy was a diminutive woman with short-cropped salt-and-pepper hair and a friendly manner. These assistants were an important segment of the medical hierarchy at the Hutch, with more training and specialization than nurses; many of them were, in fact, former nurses.

They explained that my chemotherapy would begin the following day. I would take my first chemotherapy drug, busulfan, in an oral dose every few hours for the next four days. There would be a day of rest, then two doses of the second drug, Cytoxan, which I would get intravenously for two consecutive days. I would be carefully monitored and given plenty of other drugs to combat the near-lethal toxicity of the regimen.

The Hickman catheter dangling from my chest was soon hooked up to the intravenous pole that would be my constant companion for the next two months, with several little pumps that would keep the drugs and fluids flowing into my body. The rhythmic little beeps of those pumps would become the soundtrack for my stay here, twenty-four hours a day.

The transplant ward had a cook who took food orders, since the things patients could or would eat were over the map. Usually, after the chemotherapy and radiation, patients became too nauseated to eat solid food. I didn't know it yet, but I would soon have no interest whatsoever in eating. I had a light dinner of roast chicken and rice the first night, and for hospital food it was not bad at all. My family and Deborah left about 9:30, and I fell asleep soon afterward, trying to blank out the anxiety I felt about the chemotherapy blitzkrieg scheduled to begin early the next morning.

My mother arrived at 8 A.M., in time to sit with me as I got my "loading dose" of Dilantin, an anticonvulsant given to prevent the neurological side effects of the chemotherapy drug busulfan. As the intravenous line was hooked to my catheter, the nurse explained that Dilantin had side effects of its own: vertigo, dizziness, flushing, oral numbness, headache, and nausea. I would also be getting continuous intravenous doses of another drug called Zofran, as part of a study of its usefulness in combating nausea.

Twenty minutes later, the "team" made its visit. I would soon get used to this morning hospital ritual, which typically started at about 8 A.M. when a small posse of white-coated doctors, physician's assistants, and other members of the transplant team, including visiting doctors from as far away as Brazil and India, arrived in my room to have a look at me and update the file on my condition.

The lead physician that month was Dr. Jean Sanders, a woman with short blond hair and a southern drawl who looked to be in her early fifties. Often brusque, she also had a pretty good sense of humor, which helped, since I felt not unlike a lab specimen, as in a huddle they all peered at me over their clipboards and scribbled notes before vanishing out the door as quickly as they had come in.

The good news that first morning was that my blood tests showed that I had no traces of the herpes simplex virus in my system, a problem that many other patients had. That meant I wouldn't need intravenous doses of yet another drug, acyclovir. We talked for a while about my nutritional needs, and how my calorie count would be maintained through intravenous liquids called "total parenteral nutrition," or TPN, after I could no longer stand real food.

"So, how many calories are we talking about here?" I asked. "Enough to maintain your weight at its current level," the nutritionist on the team replied. I thought about this for a minute. "What about giving me enough calories to maintain the weight of someone weighing a few pounds less than me?" I suggested. Though I wasn't overweight at 128 pounds, I figured that if I was going to be as sick as a dog and not get to eat, I might as well have a sylphlike figure to show for it.

But this was not in the program. The nutritionist explained that even heavier patients were maintained at their regular weight during transplant. Patients couldn't afford the potential loss of muscle mass, or any "wasting" during transplant, and they needed the nutrients in all the calories they would be getting. I would be encouraged to exercise as much as possible by walking around the corridors and eventually would get physical therapy to build back muscle tone.

I didn't have long to grouse about my caloric intake and my muscle tone. At 10 A.M., the nurses brought in my first dose of busulfan, five huge transparent gelatin capsules with six tiny white pills inside each. I gritted my teeth, grabbed a big glass of water, and began methodically swallowing them, one at a time. It took about fifteen minutes to get them all down, but I did it. "Now I know what they mean by horse pills," I remarked to my mother.

A half hour later, I hadn't yet felt any ill effects. I took a phone call from Steven Robert, a good friend back in New York who had promised to keep me up to date on all the gossip and goings-on. I had some tea and crackers. A nurse gave me some antibiotic drugs, Bactrim and fluconazole, to swallow. My father, Chris, and Deborah hung around, watching videos with me and talking about books we'd read. We listened to Beethoven's "Eroica" and Paul Simon's "Graceland" on the CD player. It was almost like a normal afternoon at home.

About two forty-five, Mary Brown, a research nurse, came in to talk to me about the study drug Zofran, and warned me that it might give me a bad headache. Sure enough, a few hours later, after I gulped down my third dose of busulfan capsules, my head began to throb, almost as if someone were hitting me in the head with a hammer. I could hardly bear the bright sun filtering in through the windows, but I didn't want to shut out my view, so I put on a pair of sunglasses.

At about 5 P.M. Schiffman came in to do a spinal tap, which was necessary to see if the leukemia cells were present in the cerebrospinal fluid. She gave me a sedative called Ativan that was soon to become one of my favorite drugs. I was so intent on the pain in my head that I barely noticed the fact that a needle was being pushed into my spine.

That night, with the help of more sedatives, I drifted off to sleep around midnight. But at about three in the morning, I woke up to the blare of what sounded like a fire alarm. I lurched up in my bed, realizing that the sound of a clanging bell was in my own head. A wave of nausea washed over me, and I started to make my way to the bathroom, forgetting until it tugged at my breast that my catheter was hooked to the IV pole. With my head pounding I grabbed the pole and started wheeling it toward the bathroom, making it there just in time to heave into the sink. As wave after wave of nausea washed over me, I threw up again and again, and when there was nothing left, dry heaved for a few minutes more.

Staggering back to the bed, I fell into it. I finally had a taste of what I was in for.

EIGHT

COUNTDOWN TO GROUND ZERO

N ow that I was in the hospital, the loss of control really hit me. I felt powerless, totally dependent upon others, the way a hostage must feel toward a captor. After a while, you can't imagine what it would be like not to be in captivity. As a transplant patient, you are told what to do and what not to do, you have virtually no privacy, and your day is filled with the rituals of medication and medical procedure. They give you drugs, then give you drugs to fight the side effects of the drugs, and more drugs to counter the side effects of those drugs.

Though I had swallowed the first dose of busulfan pills easily enough, each subsequent dose was harder and harder to get down. By the end of Day Two, I would look at my pile of pills and wonder how I was going to choke even one down. At night, the duty nurse would rouse me twice from my fitful sleep to take the busulfan capsules. If the pills came up as soon as I swallowed them, which they often did, the nurse would kindly but firmly make me take them again.

I was nauseous and dizzy most of the time. During the day I tried to focus on anything but what I was feeling. I stayed on the phone with Alix Freedman and other people at the office, discussing stories with reporters and talking with my deputy, Dennis

Kneale, about various and sundry things going on at work. In the morning, I tried to choke down some cereal and fruit but usually managed just some tea. Coffee, my usual morning beverage of choice, suddenly turned my stomach.

The hospital staff tried as best as they could to explain what was going to happen to me. One physician's assistant told me, "It's as if we are giving you AIDS, but you will get your immune system back eventually." Explaining the effect of the chemotherapy by equating it with the AIDS virus seemed strange to me, but when you thought about it, the comparison was apt.

No matter how many times you hear that nausea and vomiting are side effects of your treatment, no one can actually describe to you what it's like to feel that way most of the time. After my first night, I knew I was lucky to have even made it as far as the bathroom. The nurses provided me with a large, pink plastic basin that was never more than arm's reach away. Sometimes I just sat there with it on my lap, waiting. It was often a relief just to get it over with because throwing up temporarily halted the nausea.

Though I was to be cared for by nurses over three shifts a day, the daytime nurses were assigned several patients each so there would be someone to call for and some sense of individual care. My nurse was Margaret Verbois, a gentle, unflappable divorced mother with a daughter in college; she instantly hit it off with my mother. She was the kind of person who exuded calm, which was a good thing to have around there. But all the nurses were wonderful; one of my favorites was Pam Conyers, in her twenties and several months into a pregnancy. One day as she hooked up my medications, she told me the story of how she had survived leukemia as a teenager and had wanted to work with leukemia patients herself.

On Friday, July 18, I finally swallowed my last dose of busulfan, and looked forward to my day of "rest." To my surprise, the team told me I was doing well enough to leave the hospital for a few hours with my family and friends before I came back for round two of my chemotherapy, the intravenous Cytoxan. Nancy had arrived in Seattle to spend a few days, and came to the hospital with my brother and Deb to fetch me. I was unhooked from my intravenous pole, took a shower, dressed in real clothes, and walked out into the warm July morning, like a prisoner let out of solitary.

We took a drive around town; it was one of those beautiful days in Seattle where, from a hill above the city, you could see Mount Rainier to the south, the Cascades to the east, and the Olympic Peninsula to the west, all in a sweeping panorama. We spent the afternoon at the Marriott sitting on our big wraparound terrace, enjoying the cloudless summer day, watching seaplanes land on Lake Union as sailboats wafted by in a regatta. We prepared a big barbecue with swordfish, corn on the cob, and baked potatoes, though all I could manage when it came time to eat was a potato.

The respite was short-lived. By 8 P.M., my headache was hammering at me again, and by the time I got back to the hospital the pain was so intolerable the night duty physician's assistant ordered a dose of morphine. It took the headache away, and allowed me to sleep. The research nurse who was studying Zofran had asked me not to take any more of the sedative Ativan because it interfered with her study, so I hadn't gotten much sleep in the previous two days.

I began walking around the hospital corridors with one of my family members in tow. We would wheel my IV pole with us as we looked into the rooms of other patients and occasionally stopped to chat with someone in the hall. Patients were discouraged from getting too close to one another because any infection one got could be passed easily to another.

I usually tried to be out of the room when the cleaning staff came around to swab the decks with an overpowering disinfectant that burned my nose and made me gag. When I was in the room, everyone else had to wear yellow paper masks. If I left the room, I had to wear the mask. For the high-risk patients and those with unrelated matches in the isolation rooms it was much worse; plastic curtains separated them from everyone else. Mothers couldn't touch their sick children without wearing sanitized hospital gowns and latex gloves.

My mother, with her nursing experience and naturally sympathetic demeanor, was often sought out for advice or help by the mothers of the young children in the ward as we took our laps around the floor. One whole section of the ward was reserved for tiny infants, some as young as two months old. It was hard to look into their rooms and see them hooked up to respirators, tubes, and oxygen masks, their tiny bodies racked by the drugs and disease. Many of them didn't have much of a chance at survival, and had been taken on as patients by Fred Hutchinson after being told elsewhere there was nothing to do. One afternoon as we walked past one room, we heard horrible wrenching sobs as the mother of a six-month-old boy was told he had just died. "At least I've had almost forty years," I told Deborah. "He never had a chance to live."

But there were babies who were doing okay, whose lives the bone marrow transplants would save. There was little Princess, a one-year-old black girl with big brown eyes who wailed in pain and fear at the things that were happening to her, but would just as suddenly laugh and smile at a new toy or a funny face Chris made through the doorway. And there was Michael, a beautiful toddler whose little eyebrows were always arched, his blue eyes opened wide, quizzically, as if to say, "What's going on?" Michael was in the middle of radiation treatments, and the nurses would wrap him in a blue blanket, sit him up in one of the red Radio Flyer wagons, and wheel him down to the radiation room.

Dr. Storb stopped by often to look in on me, though he wasn't on service that month; it helped me feel better to know he was watching out for me. He would distract me by telling me about a weekend hike in the mountains or his latest triumph in a single scull race across Puget Sound. Modest as he was, he was very competitive. He was proud of the fact that he regularly beat rivals in their twenties in those races. Another frequent visitor was University of Washington scientist Alex Fefer, who came in one day to tell me he had just met my friend Patti Matson and her husband Ed Gottesman at a party in New York and had promised to look in on me. Dr. Fefer had been part of the original bone marrow transplant team with Thomas and Storb, and was full of interesting stories and insights. Sadly, my Dad had to leave us to go back to his business in Pittsburgh for a while.

On the wall in my hospital room, the team put up a chart called "Laura's Count Worksheet," the daily progress report on every aspect of my blood and my immune system. There was a column for my white blood cell count, which would show what was happening to my overall immune system. Then there was the measure of my "polys," the granulocytes that fight infection, and the "bands," which were the immature polys. Another column tracked my absolute neutrophil count, or ANC, which was the polys and bands added together and comprised the fighting force of the immune system. After that was the platelet column, which showed the level of the cells that formed clots and stopped bleeding, and finally, my hematocrit, the percentage of red blood cells in my plasma.

The worksheet was like the countdown to ground zero. It started on July 14, Day minus 8. As the chemotherapy began its assault on my body, the numbers all went in the opposite direction of where they were supposed to be normally. My white blood cell count started to plunge downward—my polys, my bonds, my ANC count—as did my hematocrit and platelets.

As the numbers headed south, I began to feel sicker and weaker. My hands began to shake all the time and I couldn't hold a pen steady enough to write anything legible. But I often would wake up at two or three in the morning and talk into a tape recorder to keep myself company and keep track of what was happening to me. In the wee hours of July 17, the last day of the busulfan dose, I tried to talk myself into a better frame of mind.

"Just took a big dose of the little pills, and you're not going to throw up because it's too hard to swallow them again. . . . Think serene, peaceful, cool images. . . . Your body is here being cured, but you are somewhere else. Anywhere but here."

Trying to visualize myself somewhere else was a mental trick I started using often. An executive I knew from reporting on the movie business, Dawn Steel, had given me a book about "creative visualization," which sounded like a lot of bunk to me at first. But there was something to it: I found that when I had to I could use my mind not just to tough it out, but to try to escape what was happening to me. I covered the walls in my hospital room with pictures of all my favorite places: images as diverse as the wildflowers on the lower slopes of Mount Rainier, the lush palms in the back garden of the Beverly Hills Hotel as seen from the terrace of a room I often had stayed in, and a beautiful sandy beach on Long Island. I would stare at one of the photographs, close my eyes, and just envision myself walking into the picture.

In the middle of these escapes, I would often open my eyes, grab my pink basin, and throw up. I found myself worrying into my tape recorder: "What happens if you throw up when you're sleeping? Isn't that what happened to Jimi Hendrix and Janis Joplin?" I tried to give myself little pep talks: "You gotta just hunker down there . . . the best visualization is Mount Rainier. Think of those fields, flowers . . . better to keep your eyes shut."

But it was hard to run away completely. I was put on heavy intravenous doses of fluids to keep my body hydrated and prepare me for the next chemotherapy drug, Cytoxan, which I got on July 19 and 20, in two intravenous infusions lasting an hour and forty-five minutes each. The extra water made me feel like I was going to burst, and I complained to my mother that I felt "puffy." Another catheter was inserted into my bladder to "irrigate" me. I was put on Bactrim, an antibacterial drug, to ward off a potentially fatal lung infection from a parasite.

Great. So now I was lying in bed with my head exploding, a poisonous substance flowing into my body, a painful catheter jammed into my urethra, fluids pumping me up, and still vomiting every half hour or so. On top of this I got violent hiccups. I was able to control them with my tried-and-true strategy of sitting very still while holding my breath for twenty seconds. It actually worked, a small triumph. Thanks to a dose of Benadryl, the antihistamine I was now being given along with the sedative Ativan to help me sleep, I dozed off for a few hours.

I had a dream that I was at a party in New York with hundreds of people, trying to hide my catheter and the bag of urine attached to it. Finally, I found a Bergdorf's shopping bag to stick it in, and slung the bag over my arm. Just as the bag burst in my dream, I woke up with a start, feeling as if I had three full bladders instead of one. My mother summoned the nurse, who told me the only thing I could do was to stand up and turn around a little to relieve the pressure and empty my bladder into the bag.

By 10 P.M. my tubes were leaking and had to be changed. I had to stand up every few minutes to keep my bladder emptying through the catheter, and all the movement was making me nauseous again. I finally persuaded my mother to go home at about 11 P.M. At one point I think I actually slept standing up and leaning against my bed.

The next morning, as usual, Mom was back before 9 A.M., taking her meticulous notes. "Bladder draining. Not taking much by mouth; needs distraction; watching movie. Would you believe *Gidget Goes to Rome?* Dr. Storb in; reassuring; told her to rest; doesn't have to do anything today if not up to it. Got half of last dose of Bactrim down. Dozing. Wants to wash; refuses bedbath; Margaret unplugged her and she took a quick shower. Movement causes nausea and a bit of wretching but no vomiting."

That afternoon, with a second dose of Cytoxan finished, the nausea became worse, the constant bladder pressure almost unbearable. The Zofran that was supposed to combat some of the side effects of all this clearly wasn't working, and the headaches it gave me were unbearable. I had agreed to take it as part of a study, but now I asked to be taken off of it.

At most research hospitals, patients will be asked to participate in studies like this one; some don't carry much risk to the patient and will benefit future patients, which is a good thing to be a part of if you can. But you do need to closely study the risks and possible side effects; if you aren't up to scrutinizing them yourself, have a family member do it for you. Some studies are randomized, which means researchers will basically toss a coin to see whether you get a new drug or a placebo. You may not feel too comfortable with that procedure, since usually you won't actually know which way the coin toss went for you. But if you feel a new treatment being researched offers benefits for you, by all means go for the study. You will have to sign an informed consent, but it isn't a binding contract. The forms also tell you that you remain free to withdraw that consent at any time.

After I withdrew from the Zofran study, I decided the best thing would be to simply rely on the other antinausea drugs the hospital already had in its regular protocol. There was quite an array of such medications for pain, nausea, and sleeplessness, some of which worked better for some people than others. I tried them all in various combinations. "Trying not to lose heart," I whispered into my tape recorder at three in the morning one day. "I try to suck on a little orange Popsicle to get the horrible taste out of my mouth but even that makes me sick. They're trying different combinations of drugs to help stop the pain and nausea—morphine, Compazine, Thorazine—it's like mixing cocktails, but this ain't no party."

On July 21, the day before the transplant, my hair, as promised, began to fall out. I was horrified yet fascinated by it, staring at myself in the mirror as I pulled out huge clumps with a mere tug. Deborah tried to brush it for me, but it came out in her hands. I swept back what was left into a wide headband and decided to see what happened. The good news was that the bladder catheter was coming out at last, and all the fluids pumping into me would stop. The Cytoxan was finished. I slept fitfully between bouts of throwing up green bile.

On July 22, transplant day arrived. Chris checked in, and was sent straight to pre-op, where the anesthesiologist put him under at about 10 A.M. By 11 A.M., a tube was pushed down his throat to keep him breathing, and a team of doctors and nurses were leaning over him, starting the painstaking procedure of extracting his precious marrow. Using long, powerful surgical needles, they made a dozen holes in the skin over the bone mass that made up his iliac crest, the hip bones, which contain one of the body's best deposits of bone marrow. Then, over the next two hours, they inserted the needles under the skin into the bone about 300 times to suck out two quarts of bone marrow and blood—or about 2 percent of the marrow in Chris's body. Luckily, he could spare that much; his body would regenerate the difference in about four weeks.

Meanwhile, I was sent to the X-ray department to make sure my lungs were clear. The chemotherapy had attacked the abnormal cells that were invading my body, but as expected, it had also completely knocked out my immune system. My white blood cell count was drifting further down each day and I wasn't making any new immature cells, or bands. Only the drugs protected me from a deadly infection, and in a few days there would be nothing to stop me from bleeding to death. Without the marrow I was about to get from Chris, I would soon have died.

That very day, the patient in room 1019, the big one my mother had been keeping her eye on, was discharged. Over the hour that I was in the X-ray unit, my mother and Deborah mobilized a couple of the Radio Flyer wagons and a trolley and relocated everything from my small room into this large one. I came back just as they had everything arranged, and collapsed onto the bed in my spacious new quarters. Though we lost our view of Mount Rainier, this room was more than twice the size of the first, including a large anteroom, much more privacy and quiet, and a stunning view of downtown Seattle, Puget Sound, and the distant mountains of the Olympic Peninsula.

At noon, Dr. Storb came in to check up on me, and a moment later, Kathy Schiffman, the physician's assistant, came in to announce, "Chris is in the recovery room and the procedure went great." But she explained that there would have to be a slight delay in the transplant while they "washed" the red blood cells out of Chris's marrow. Even though our tissue types were an identical match, our blood types were "ABO incompatible"; his blood type was A-positive and mine was type O.

If the red blood cells were left in the blood that would come along with Chris's marrow when I received it, natural antibodies that remained in my own blood might gang up on my brother's cells. Those cells would be destroyed and their contents excreted through my kidneys, which would quickly clog up, possibly leading to kidney failure. This could all be avoided by removing those cells. Once his marrow had migrated into my bones, and was accepted by my body, it would start producing its own kind of white cells, red cells, and platelets, so my blood type would convert to Chris's.

For the next three hours, as I waited for Chris, I drifted in and out of sleep. As my mother watched me and checked on Chris's progress, she spoke by phone to my father and my brother Art, and wrote in her spiral notebook: "Half the most important people in the world to me are here in this hospital and an ordeal I wouldn't wish on an enemy has taken over my entire existence. The universe feels tilted. Sometimes Laura says she can't do this . . . but she is actually doing it."

At 5 P.M., Kathy Schiffman pushed Chris through my doorway in a wheelchair. He was carrying a small plastic bag filled with marrow and blood—and my new life. As a nurse hung it on the intravenous pole, Chris, still groggy from the anesthesia, was struggling to stay awake. "I wanted to deliver this personally," he said with a big smile. We held hands as the nurse opened the In valve on my catheter, and turned on the pump. With my mother and Deborah, we watched as the liquid slowly ran down the tubing and disappeared into my body.

"Marrow started!" my mother scribbled. "A small procedure that is the most momentous occasion in her life—there should be drum rolls, a fanfare—a parade—but there is just the beep of our ever-present pump, delivering the goods!"

Now that it was finally happening, it seemed miraculous, unfathomable—this tiny bit of marrow would swim into my bloodstream, find its way into the cavities of my largest bones, get settled in, and if all went according to plan, "engraft," and start growing me a whole new supply of blood cells and a new immune system. We called it the Mighty Marine Marrow. It had to work.

Chris stayed with me for an hour, but finally dozed off in his wheelchair. As my mother wheeled him back to his room, he roused himself for a minute to look back at me. I thought maybe he was going to say something serious, but he smiled, and advised, "If you feel like doing calisthenics in the morning, just ignore the urge until it goes away."

Over the next hour, the staff watched carefully for complications that sometimes arise as the new marrow flows into the body—fever, chills, hives, chest pains. But by seven-forty the last precious drop had disappeared into my catheter without incident.

The transplant was completed. Now the hard part would begin.

NINE

A NEW BIRTHDAY

In transplant terms, July 22 was the first day of the rest of my new life. It was a virtual rebirth, my second "birthday." There was, however, no guarantee of surviving this second infancy.

All those complications I had read about, all the plagues that could still ravage my body, were about to come and get me. The pain, nausea, and vomiting I was experiencing were merely a sneak preview of what was in store.

I stopped even trying to eat food, which meant my sole nutrition was the liquid diet which until now had been given just as a supplement. Margaret, my nurse, hung a bag of milky white fluid on my IV pole, explaining it contained all the fats, proteins, and carbohydrates I would need. The medical team came in at about 10 A.M. on July 23, massing in my doorway to congratulate me on the transplant and tell me about all the new drugs I would be taking to combat the various bacterial, fungal, and viral infections that were now a danger while Chris's bone marrow established a beachhead.

To protect against rejection and graft-versus-host disease, I was given the antirejection drug cyclosporine, the chemotherapy agent methotrexate, and immunoglobulin, a human antibody preparation they hoped would reduce the incidence and severity of GVH. The chemotherapy, as expected, had knocked out my ovarian function, and I began taking hormone replacement drugs to keep me from going into early menopause.

So far, I had been handling things relatively well. Deborah and I even agreed to participate in a coping skills study being conducted by Janet Abrams, the staff psychologist. She was researching the short- and long-term emotional effects of being a transplant patient, and of taking care of one. We regularly filled out forms asking us questions on everything from how we were feeling about life, the future, and each other, to whether we sometimes felt isolated and misunderstood. I didn't mind participating in that kind of study; it didn't involve taking drugs and it helped us understand that what we were feeling was normal.

But the drugs soon started having a strange effect on me. Droperidol, one of the antinausea medications, was making me feel stir-crazy and antsy, and I had a strange sensation of wanting to get out of my skin, to break free of the prison of my own body. I also experienced a feeling of dread, as if I knew that things were about to take a turn for the worse. Twice in the space of one day I asked the nurse to unhook me from the IV pole for a half hour so I could walk around the hospital ward, in an effort to shake the negative feeling.

"I just want to get out of here," I told my mother on July 24, two days after the transplant. "I want my life back." I had virtually no privacy, and precious little dignity. I longed just for the little things I had always taken for granted—being able to get up, exercise, jump in the shower, put on makeup, wash and dry my hair. Transplant patients were not allowed to receive any plants or flowers, the usual things that can cheer up a hospital room, for fear that some spores or bacteria might cause a problem.

I also felt like a guinea pig in a cage. Every time I threw up or went to the bathroom, someone took the proceeds away to be examined, as if reading tea leaves, to see what it might portend. In the bathroom, the toilet was covered with a plastic basin divided in half. Complying with its purpose was not so easy, especially with female anatomy. "I keep pooping in the pee cup and peeing in the poop cup," I apologized to the nurse.

Chris, limping slightly with pain, was released from the hospital the day after the transplant, and came in to my room in street clothes to show us the huge white bandage covering his entire lower back. He said it hurt a little, and Mom changed the dressing for him. We put on Motown music and actually danced around the room for a few minutes. Suddenly Art walked in the door—he had come back from Connecticut as a surprise to spend a few days with us. I was so happy to see him, for a few minutes I actually forgot how bad I felt.

But that didn't last long. All the systems in my body were starting to go haywire in the aftermath of the chemotherapy. Chemo kills fast-growing cells, which is the reason it is effective in killing cancer cells and also why it makes your hair fall out. But at the high doses a transplant patient receives, it also wreaks havoc with other cells and tissues. It was as if the inner lining of my throat, esophagus, and stomach were sloughing off, causing excruciating pain. Now when I threw up, it was like vomiting fire. I wasn't eating anything, but bile was constantly churning in my stomach that had to be expelled. It made me feel for all the world like Linda Blair in *The Exorcist.*

And the constant vomiting made my throat so raw it felt as if a wolf had its fangs in my neck. Margaret sprayed some lidocaine, a topical anesthetic, in my throat, but that only made me more nauseous. There was no escape and no relief. My father, after years of back problems, had a favorite saying: "Happiness is the absence of pain." Now I knew exactly what he meant. "Isn't there something else they could give me to stop this?" I whimpered to my mother on the third day after the transplant, July 25.

My mother went out to lobby my case with the physician's assistant. A couple of hours later, two doctors arrived from the pain and toxicity unit; their mission was to study pain and to figure out how to alleviate it. They sat at the foot of my bed, where I gazed balefully at them and asked, "Which one of you is Pain and which is Toxicity?"

One problem was that the most effective painkiller, morphine, was making me so violently ill each time I took it that I threw up blood. They suggested we try a milder drug called Dilaudid. It proved not to be as effective as morphine, but at least it didn't make me sicker. I was able to administer the painkiller to myself by pushing a button; you could only get so much at a time, so there was no danger of overdose.

They also tried the drug Marinol, a synthetic version of the compound found in marijuana that was being widely used to help chemotherapy patients. I didn't like it one bit. I had smoked marijuana in high school, but I grew to dislike the spacey way it made me feel and the weird, paranoid, dry-mouthed feeling it gave me, and this stuff had pretty much the same effect.

The next week was a blur of pain and misery. The chemotherapy, and probably the antirejection drug methotrexate, had thrown my salivary glands out of whack, and I developed a bad case of mucositis, a severe irritation and ulceration of the mouth. At one point I was making no saliva; my mouth felt so dehydrated I had to constantly rinse it out with water to keep it from drying up completely. But water couldn't quench the thirst of my tissues, which were dried out from the inside. A few days later things went in the opposite direction, and I was producing so much saliva that I had to have a special device in my mouth to constantly suction out the excess fluid so I didn't drown myself. "This really sucks," I told my mother, laughing weakly.

Though the pain medications made me feel drowsy and dimwitted, I was getting very little actual sleep. "There's this new device next to my bed now," I said into the tape recorder at 2 A.M. "It looks like the hookah from *Alice in Wonderland* . . . it allows you to suck mucus from inside your throat, which goes into some hidden little bag to be disposed of by proper authorities . . . I'm getting the hang of it."

I tried like hell to keep up at work. I had an extra phone line installed next to my bed for my laptop computer, and I read all the stories my reporters were filing. Often, I would talk to the reporters, giving them ideas, suggesting people to call, angles to investigate. Johnnie Roberts, the senior reporter on my staff covering the entertainment industry, was in the midst of a big story, and one night we talked for a half hour, although for the life of me I can't remember what it was about. "Talking at length with Johnnie Roberts," my mother noted one night in her journal at about 8 P.M. "Serious business . . . important stuff . . . very involved and detailed." That's my only recollection.

Even with my shaky hands, I would sometimes try to take notes, thinking I was writing things down legibly. When I looked at the paper afterward, I would see lines scrawled over each other, sentences running off the page, indecipherable scribbles. But keeping the connection to work was one of the most important things for me. Every few days I would get a Federal Express package with mail and all the trade magazines, and I would plow through the papers, Wall Street analysts' reports, and publications like *Variety*.

While it was easy enough to leaf through magazines and newspapers, it was almost impossible to concentrate on reading a book. Instead, I almost always had a movie on in the background; I had a veritable library of tapes that had been sent by sympathetic executives at some of the movie studios I covered. Though I initially balked at accepting the dozens of tapes that kept pouring in, I figured it would be okay if I donated them to the hospital. The nurses set up a cabinet in which to store all of them, and they proved to be a big hit with the other patients. Someone was always wandering by to see if anything new had come in. We had everything from *Breakfast at Tiffany's* to *Saturday Night Fever*.

My brothers stocked the room with compact discs, supplemented by the occasional package from friends like Bob Zito, a public relations executive who was then working for Sony. I liked to listen to upbeat dance and hip-hop music, rock and roll, and serious classical stuff. At one point, three different friends sent a copy of a CD by Enya, the New Age chanteuse whose music was a big hit that summer. That also was a favorite among the hospital staff, who would often come in and ask if we could play it for them. It had an eerie, almost funereal sound—and drove me completely nuts. But all the entertainment at least gave my family some pleasant distractions.

I continued to take my walks and occasionally ride the exercise bike in my room. Deborah started taking me down to the physical therapy department, which had exercise mats and machines and a nice therapist who helped me do leg lifts and arm exercises. I felt so weak, however, that it was hard to exercise for long.

By now it had been more than a month since I arrived in Seattle, and I had seen hardly anyone outside of my close inner circle. In truth, it was hard to imagine having to face anyone else. But one day I got a call from Herbert Allen, an investment banker I had known for more than a decade, someone I considered a good friend. He announced he planned to be in Seattle and wanted to drop in. I was touched that he was thinking of me and told him to come on by. Just before he arrived, I gathered what little hair I had under a wide headband, and tried to look presentable.

My mother, Chris, and Deborah went to lunch to give us some time alone to catch up, and we chatted for a half hour or so. But suddenly I felt the familiar waves of nausea washing over me. "Please don't let me throw up in front of Herbert," I prayed. But it was worse than that. Seeing that I was about to grab for my pink basin, he jumped up and grabbed it for me, thrusting it under my face. He got to me just in time for me to throw up all over his arm. He tried to make a joke of it: "That's the effect I have on all the girls," he laughed. But I was absolutely mortified.

"A nice visit for her in spite of puking on the guy," my mother jotted in her notebook after he left.

That afternoon, in the shower, more of my hair washed down the drain. Finally, I couldn't stand it anymore. "Can we just shave it off?" I asked Jenny, one of the nurses, first thing the next morning. "Absolutely, whenever you want," she said. "How about right now?" I answered. She left and came back a few minutes later with a big electric razor. As my mother documented the whole thing with her camera, the razor buzzed neatly over my head. First she mowed off the top, making me look like Larry from the Three Stooges, and then she neatly finished off the fringe that remained at the base of my skull.

"You have a beautiful head," my mother assured me. "Just like Sinead O'Connor," Deborah chimed in. Great. Now I looked like a bald Irish singer best known for disrespecting the pope.

Art and Chris came in as the last of my hair was being swept up, and both came over immediately to rub my head and pose for a picture. Now I had even less hair than Chris, who kept his in a regulation "high and tight" crew cut. "I figured if I had Marine marrow, I might as well look like a Marine," I told him. Chris had spent the previous two afternoons at a nearby military base fulfilling his monthly reserve duty requirement, and he lent me his officer's beret, which I perched on my bald pate. Deb rushed out to Nordstrom's in downtown Seattle and came back with a half-dozen beautiful scarves, which we practiced wrapping around my head.

I decided I wanted to do something radical—go outside. It was a beautiful warm evening, still sunny, and no one had said I couldn't venture out. I put a bandanna around my head and covered it with a baseball hat; I donned a yellow paper mask to cover my nose and mouth; sunglasses completed the disguise. I looked like the Invisible Man. With Art and Chris clutching me under either arm, I stepped onto the elevator, and walked through the hospital lobby to the main exit. We strolled around the grounds, then rested on a bench in a little parklike area. As I sat hunched next to my two brothers, I couldn't help comparing our very different physical conditions. While they were strong and healthy, I felt like the runt of the litter.

We came back upstairs a few minutes later, only to learn that another of the ward's beautiful infants, little Tyler, had died. Everyone had been rooting for him so hard; his young parents had been like frightened ghosts haunting the hallways for weeks. As my mother told me what had happened, I started to cry, but my own tears just made me throw up again. Nausea seemed to be my body's answer to every emotion.

The next day, a package arrived with a videotape from Nancy and another high school chum, Vicky Klarich. I had just missed my twentieth high school reunion, but there it was, on video, with everyone waving into the camera and saying, "Hi, Laura! We miss you! Wish you were here! Get well soon!" Nearly everyone I remembered from Fair Lawn High School was there, looking pretty good after all these years. Good thing they couldn't see me now, I thought.

I drifted off to sleep, waking up at three in the morning to go to the bathroom. Concentrating on the now familiar task of maneuvering my IV pole into the tiny space between the sink and the toilet, I flipped on the overhead light, caught sight of myself in the mirror, and gasped. I was bald, my skin was yellow, and the constant retching had broken so many blood vessels in my eyes that the whites were nearly all red. There were purple circles rimming my eyes, bruises from the trauma on the muscles around the eyeballs, which would bulge out of my head when I threw up. It was so awful, there was nothing I could do but laugh at myself. "Hey, good-looking," I said to my image. "Just get back from Auschwitz?"

Back in bed, I drifted in and out of sleep, but woke up about 4:30 A.M. when the night nurse came to take my vital signs and promised to get me some more antinausea medication. "It's hard to put words to the kind of pain you're in . . . it feels like someone put a stake in my throat and I'm swallowing around it," I said to my only companion, the tape recorder. "I'm coughing up blood, I'm bleeding through my nose. My body decided to have a period just to join in the fun. . . . I keep pressing this painkiller stuff, but every time I get more pain medication, it also makes me slightly nauseous, and the last thing you want to do is throw up. Please hurry back, nurse."

Dr. Abrams, the psychologist doing the study on how the patients and their caregivers were dealing with things emotionally, stopped by fairly often. She was frequently on hand to see how patients and family members were holding up. There was a great sense of family around the two transplant wards—every patient had at least one or two close relatives on hand, such as a parent or spouse. There also was a very nice chaplain who made daily rounds, stopping in now and then for a chat.

For those who didn't have a big support system, the Hutch bent over backward to help out. Social workers were available to assist with housing, transportation, and financial aid, and to make arrangements between children's schools back home and the Hutch school for patients and their siblings. They provided things like letters to airlines so people could make quick flight arrangements without paying high prices, and they were available to run interference with employers. There were family support meetings, and constant activities to give caregivers a break from the hospital. Local groups sometimes donated baseball or concert tickets.

I knew I was lucky to have my family so close to me, but sometimes I just needed to shut them all out. "There's a sense of alienation between you and anyone related to you even though they are as close to you as they've ever been," I said into my tape recorder in one 3 A.M. session. "You don't want to push them away at a time like this, but sometimes you have to."

Still, Abrams told my mother she thought I was doing remarkably well emotionally, and my mother was encouraged too. "Laura's laid-back and on an even keel today," she wrote in her notebook. "No big emotional highs or lows but an acceptance of the events as they happen . . . she makes an adjustment at each new level of events . . . and the humor is always present and breaks out in spite of whatever developments occur."

At least, that was the way I *tried* to deal with it. There was nothing to do but tackle things one day at a time, to try to see the humor in it all. "What new plagues can I expect?" I asked the medical team when they came in on the morning of July 29.

Quite a few, as it turned out.

TEN

STIR-CRAZY

On Thursday, July 30, eight days after the transplant, my new marrow wasn't yet making enough platelets, the clotting component of blood. My period had started, and I was bleeding heavily; without platelets, there was a danger of bleeding to death. Chris, as my marrow donor, could also give me some of his platelets. But I would need far more than he could spare, so the team decided to supplement what Chris was giving me with platelets from anonymous donors in the local blood bank.

The heavy bleeding gave me severe pelvic cramps, and this came at the same time that the pain in my throat had reached the point of being unbearable. The pain team, or the Pain Tox Dox, as we were calling them by now, increased the amount of painkiller I could administer to myself, and I was hitting that button like a pinball machine, although I was still only able to get as much medication as the computerized system allowed me. But while the painkillers worked for a while, they inevitably contributed to my violent retching and vomiting.

My mother ran out to a drugstore for a hot water bottle for my cramps—the hospital had no such low-tech remedy in stock—and constantly applied ice packs to my throat. She was calm, soothing, seemingly in control all the time. But she wrote in her notebook, "If there is a feeling worse than the one which consumes you while watching your child suffer, I do not want to experience it . . . she will recover from this devastation . . . SHE WILL."

Then, the combination of the pain medication and the anonymous donor platelets started to have a bizarre effect on me. I felt suddenly as if I were in some other dimension, out in the Twilight Zone somewhere. I began experiencing shaking, chills, uncontrollable tremors. I was barely able to get out of bed to take the daily shower that had become a refuge to me, a sanctuary, in which I could sit on a bench in the stall and let the warm water pour over me, lathering myself up with fragrant bath gels to escape the hospital smells. One of my closest friends, Amy Dunkin, had flown in from New York to visit for a few days, and I tried to be sociable, but it was hard to concentrate even on a simple conversation. Much of what was going on around me was becoming a blur.

A couple of days later, on August 2, my blood test showed an alarming development: my bilirubin had climbed up to seven, a dangerous number that indicated possible veno-occlusive disease of the liver. VOD, as it was known, meant that blood wasn't moving properly through the liver and kidneys—a frequent cause of death in transplant patients. My mother could barely hide her own panic, but she tried to calm herself with the knowledge that the hospital knew how to manage the situation.

"It could be a very mild form," she wrote in her notebook. "They'll manage it with careful fluid and electrolyte balance to improve the impaired flow of blood through the liver and kidneys, monitor and adjust all with drugs."

One of the problems, they had discovered, was that my liver wasn't processing the sedative Ativan and the painkiller Dilaudid, so they would have to cut back on both drugs. As they explained all this to me and described veno-occlusive disease, I remained composed, taking what I thought was careful notes. When my mother showed the illegible scrawls to me afterward, I laughed. "Who wrote this?" I asked her.

A few hours later, as the pain medication was evaporating from my system and the last of a new infusion of platelets dripped into me, I started shaking from head to toe. Blood was running down my legs in huge clots; I was suddenly very afraid, and I began crying almost hysterically. "I feel poisoned," I told my mother, who fetched Pam, the nurse on duty, and Kathy Schiffman, the physician's assistant.

They gave me a shot of Demerol to quiet the shaking, and then talked among themselves about whether my condition could be a reaction to drugs, the foreign platelets, or a combination of everything. They couldn't stop giving me platelets, or the bleeding would never stop. They would consult Dr. Sanders and the team first thing in the morning. In the meantime, Schiffman suggested that someone from the family spend the night with me.

Deborah volunteered, persuading my mother that it would be much better if she could take the night shift so my mom could get some rest and be available for the much busier daytime. She settled herself on the wide window seat, which was covered with a cushion she had purchased at a local Pier One store. My mother and Chris left, and I drifted up off to sleep, with Deborah already dozing on her makeshift bed. At ten, however, I awoke again, shaking. My teeth were chattering so badly I thought I was going to bite my tongue off, and I began hallucinating that there were things crawling on me. Over the next two hours, I ranted and raved like a drug addict in detox, trying to scratch my skin off—I just wanted to get it off me, crawl out of my skin if I could. At one point Deborah and the nurse had to physically pin me to the bed with their own bodies to keep me from hurting myself.

The next morning, Dr. Sanders conferred with my mother and Chris, and it was decided that the best thing we could do was to get my other brother Art back in Seattle, to become another platelet donor. Under ordinary circumstances, they might have had to continue using the blood bank donor platelets, and then have tried more drugs to counteract the negative effects. But we were lucky;

because Art was also a perfect bone marrow match, platelets from him would be far more compatible for me than the platelets from the donor bank.

Art had left Seattle a week earlier, and luckily, Chris reached him at home in Connecticut just as he was about to leave for a business trip to Peru. Art canceled those plans immediately and said he would be on the next plane to Seattle. Now it was his turn to come to the rescue.

I was already upset that Chris was being drained of his platelets for me; I felt like some kind of bloodsucking vampire. I started crying when they told me Art was coming back, sorry I was disrupting my brothers' lives so much. Chris hugged me and told me not even to think about it. Still, I was worried; platelet donation, we had been told, was a strain on the cardiovascular system, and they had refused to use Art as a bone marrow donor in the first place because of his irregular EKG. Wouldn't the platelet donation be a risk too? I wasn't far wrong; there was enough of a concern about just that problem that once Art got back to Seattle on Tuesday, August 4, there was a debate about whether to actually use him.

After consulting with the cardiologists and reviewing his charts again, they decided it would be okay. Again, I was lucky to have two brothers who were suitable platelet donors. Most people in my situation have to rely on platelets from the donor bank. Many don't have a bad reaction, and if they do, there are a number of drugs the hospital administers to counteract it. Unfortunately, such drugs simply add to the pharmacopoeia a transplant patient is already taking, at a point where it's better to try to reduce rather than increase drugs and their potential interactions.

For the next two weeks, Art and Chris accompanied each other daily to the blood collection center, where they were put in a room and hooked up to a cell separation device known as an apheresis machine. Needles were hooked up to the veins in both their arms; one would draw the blood out into the machine, where a centrifuge would whip out the platelets and pump the remaining blood back into the body through the intravenous needle in the opposite arm.

The procedure lasted for hours; during that time, most of their blood supply was drawn out of the body and pumped back in again, minus some platelets. When the blood came back in, it was cold, giving them bad chills, turning their lips blue, and making them weak and tired. To keep their calcium levels up and help alleviate the other bothersome symptoms, they had to eat the antacid Tums, and take iron pills to keep the levels in their blood high enough.

Art and Chris approached this trying task by looking at it as an opportunity to hang out together, to flirt with pretty nurses and crack jokes. "Tums Tums Tums Tums," they would chant, feeding them to each other until they figured out they could get the nurses to do it for them. Big wool blankets were kept warm in heated drawers Chris referred to as "pizza ovens"; they asked the nurses to tuck them into new ones every half hour or so.

Ever the macho men, they ignored doctors' suggestions that they not exercise too much for the time being. Another perk the Hutch provided to families of patients was free passes to the Seattle University gym, where Chris started working out the day after he was released from the hospital following the marrow donation surgery. He would groan and moan out loud from the pain in his back as he lifted the weights, attracting puzzled stares from other weight lifters. Now he and Art had become frequent visitors to the gym, determined to keep up their workouts. Art even tried one of his long runs, though he said the iron pills made his legs feel like lead.

In addition to supplying me with platelets, my brothers also provided heavy doses of moral support. Whenever I felt up to it, Art and Chris would take me for walks outside the hospital, usually in the early afternoon, when the sun was still warm and the traffic was light. Sometimes they just sat in the hospital room with me,

looking at a movie or reading a magazine while I lay half unconscious. Once Art was startled right out of his chair when I sat bolt
upright from a sound sleep and puked all over the place.

The shaking and chills stopped as soon as I stopped using the
anonymous platelets, and Dr. Sanders gave us some hopeful news:
it looked as if the liver problem might be resolving itself. "If you
have any veno-occlusive disease at all, it might be a very mild case,"
she told us. My bilirubin was back down to normal levels. The staff
had noticed that my bilirubin level went up whenever I had an IV
dose of the drug methotrexate, the drug I was being given along
with cyclosporine to prevent graft-versus-host disease. They short-
ened the methotrexate dose and added another drug to help calm
down what I'd come to call "that guy Billy Rubin."

On August 6, we had the first sign that this was all going to
work. Dr. Storb came in, clearly pleased, bearing the results of my
latest blood and bone marrow tests. "The marrow has engrafted,"
he told me. "You're on your way now."

What he meant was that my new marrow was starting to do its
work. The count was rising fast for my "polys," the white blood
cells that are a main fighting force in the immune system. "We have
a way to go . . . she doesn't feel as good as the numbers sound, but
that will slowly change," my mother wrote. "We all have the feeling, I hope not prematurely, that we're on the upside of this event,
knowing full well that there will be peaks and valleys . . . some of
my anxiety is lifting."

The encouraging news helped me as well. By now, I had begun
to understand that chronic, unending pain, with no hope of release,
was an impossible way to live. I had always been amazed that people would be willing to give up life itself. Meg Cox, who covered
the publishing industry at *The Wall Street Journal,* had written a
story the year before about how the Hemlock Society founder's in-
structive book *Final Exit* on different ways to kill yourself had become a bestseller. I remembered shaking my head in disbelief as I

edited that story. I simply couldn't understand at the time why people gave up and asked for assisted suicide.

But it was less difficult to comprehend now. "If I didn't think this pain was going to end, if this was not going to get better, I couldn't stand the idea of living like this," I told my mother. And talking into my tape recorder one night, I mused, "It's just too much to live with that kind of pain all the time. Part of you shuts down but the rest of you just keeps thinking, this is going to pass, time is going to pass, each minute that passes means that this is going to go away sooner."

Although it was clear from my blood counts that the transplant was beginning to work, I wasn't out of the woods yet, not by a long shot. We were soon to learn that this was a one-step-forward, two-steps-back process. The graft-versus-host disease we had spent so much time debating and worrying about began to develop, first on my skin, where strange rashes began to cover my abdomen, and then inside my stomach, which felt like a shriveled rag that had been wrung dry and left to harden in the air.

I could still barely tolerate a swallow of Jell-O, let alone eat the solid food the nutritionists felt I should be thinking about by now. Though the intense mucositis had subsided in my mouth, I always felt as if I had a block of salt dissolving on my tongue, and I had to use the suction device at least once every hour or two. "I feel like I'm living in a dentist's chair," I told my mother.

Plus, some of the drugs I was on were giving me heart palpitations and high blood pressure, which meant I had to take more drugs to combat those symptoms. And those drugs in turn gave me other symptoms—dizziness, lightheadedness, and a rapid pulse. The team felt it was time to start weaning me off intravenous drugs so I could take the medications orally. That meant swallowing pills that seemed the size of giant bullets to me. Though the nurses ground the pills and mixed them in heavy liquids like pear and apricot nectar for me to swallow, the medications just made the nectars taste foul, and if I got them down at all, I often vomited them up again.

To be sure, there were some moments of peace and calm. We watched movies on the VCR at night, laughing at old comedies like *You Can't Take It with You* and *Walk Don't Run*. But with no warning, drugs like the Dilaudid would suddenly make me feel downright psychotic. On August 7, my mother wrote that I was "shaking, running around the room, almost pulled her Hickman out of her body."

By now a new doctor, Kris Doney, had arrived to replace Dr. Sanders as head of the team for the August rotation. A younger version of Dr. Sanders, she was equally frank and straightforward, which I liked. But it was clear that none of them knew exactly what was going on with me or how to make it better. The Pain Tox Dox had now taken me off the painkiller Dilaudid and there was some thought that I might be experiencing a form of withdrawal. But the consensus seemed to be that I was having "extrapyramidal syndrome," an aberration caused by all the antinausea and pain medications I had been pumped with for the last three weeks.

Dr. Doney explained that patients have all different reactions to pain medication and antinausea drugs, depending on factors such as body weight. But sometimes reactions just couldn't be predicted. In my case, I appeared to be extra sensitive to medication and often had atypical reactions. They would decide what to do by the next day, she promised.

That night, after everyone finally left me alone, I put on a Beethoven CD and started talking to myself, into the recorder. My voice was barely a frog's croak and I had started to lose track of time.

"Well, here's a new wrinkle. August whatever-it-is, 2 A.M., and I'm experiencing the weirdest feeling. Everyone left about eleven. I was all set to go to bed, I tried a few different sleeping positions . . . then I began having these terrible feelings of anxiety and the shakes, like the D.T.'s, though it's not as bad as the other night. The nurses are all trying to figure out what's wrong with me, whether I'm just a psychopath who's finally gone off the deep end, or I took too much painkiller too long and since they took me off it this morning I'm going through withdrawal. I would do anything to make it stop. Try to be calm.

"I'm trying to use things to get myself through this; imagery, visualizing the pain as a means to a good end. But after a while you get worn down by the pain. I have all these dreams; hallucinations; I open my eyes, things are there; I close my eyes and open them again, it's gone. I've handed over the details of this to Mom; I'm not even keeping track of my counts, she writes everything down, she keeps saying it's good, it's good, it's good. It's as if I've given it up. . . . I mean I'm still here hanging in and doing everything, but I've given up all the active management, which may be just as well.

"You don't even have time to think about life, to reflect or fantasize, you are just in here thinking about what your body is going to do next. I've tried to be good, to get on the computer, to talk to the reporters about what stories they should be working on next, but it's hard, it's hard to do anything."

As I talked, I could hear the screams of one of the infants next door. "This baby next door is driving me crazy, it's constantly screaming like it's being tortured, which of course it is! I'm getting into a stir-crazy mode here where all I want is to get out of this place . . . but there's a long road ahead."

My mother, meanwhile, was writing her own thoughts: "It's easy to speak of the positive clinical picture, but the daily miseries . . . the 400 Blows, the hourly aggravating symptoms are still ever-present. It's difficult for her to feel optimistic when she can't even take a lemon candy and keep it in her stomach."

On Friday, August 7, the team agreed the best thing for now would be to discontinue everything but the Benadryl, which had the effect of counteracting the symptoms, and they also gave me a shot of a beta-blocker heart drug, Inderal, to calm me down for the night. The consensus was that Deborah should spend the night again. Neither of us were destined to get much sleep. There was nothing I could do to ward off a terrible feeling of anxiety. For nearly two hours, well past midnight, Deborah walked with me, around and around the hospital corridors, wheeling my IV pole all the time.

My mother came in the next morning to find us both bleary-eyed and exhausted. "Laura is concerned about these anxiety attacks . . . they are a frightening experience for someone who has never had such emotions . . . to have no control over feelings is disconcerting to say the least . . . but everyone is pleased with her clinical picture and the symptoms that are a plague to her WILL slowly disappear."

The next night, I was again afraid to be alone, so Deb stayed once more on her window seat. But we had a relatively peaceful night; the hysteria seemed to be over.

Over the next few days, my clinical picture continued to improve, even though I was still nauseous and vomiting all the time, and exhausted from lack of real sleep. My throat was raw from coughing, and my sinuses were blocking up. The team began to worry about signs of CMV, the cytomegalovirus that might lead to pneumonia.

On Saturday August 10, there was a distraction: a package arrived with another video, this time from Dennis Kneale, who was running my group in my absence. He had corralled the video crew from our *Wall Street Journal* television show, written a half-hour script, and cajoled twenty reporters and editors into acting in a little spoof about life at *The Wall Street Journal* without me—a depiction of utter chaos, plunging journalistic standards, and staff uprisings.

The funniest part was a scene with our buttoned-down employee benefits director, David Rosenberg, talking on the phone to a fictional insurance company representative. "Well, her doctor told her looking good is feeling good," he was saying. "You don't want to pay for the manicures?" And then, "Well, the charges, you know, she likes to stop in Harry Cipriani for a quick bite before her doctor appointment. The three-inch nail wraps? Well, she's got to fend off those doctors—they can get pretty grabby. . . . We'll see what Dow Jones can pay for and what Aetna can pay for."

On the tape was Jonathan Dahl, who I always yelled at for smelling up the area immediately outside my office with takeout Chinese food, actually eating takeout Chinese food in my office! There was Mike Waldholz, our medical writer, rushing into a meeting waving a *New England Journal of Medicine* with a supposed article on a new cure for leukemia, and Dennis thanking him and promptly depositing it in the garbage. There was Alix Freedman, Meg Cox, Suein Hwang, and Joanne Lipman in the ladies' room, complaining that all the local retailers had filed for bankruptcy after I left town. Jim Stewart, the front-page editor was there, yelling at Dennis for missing a scoop. And then there was Dennis again, tied up in his office by mutinying reporters. Even the boss, Paul Steiger, got into the act, pounding the table after he couldn't find anyone to track down a big story and yelling, "Where's Landro?"

It made me laugh and cry, and in the end, of course, all the excitement made me throw up. "How she misses it," my mother wrote in her journal that night. "She has lots of incentive to get better and get back to her great life."

The next day, Sunday, the team came bursting in as usual, full of optimism about my progress. My white blood cell count was at 1.900, and my ANC, or absolute neutrophil count, which indicated the main power of the immune system, was at an impressive 1,250. My mother was scribbling madly. "All systems are go . . . she's on her way back to her future. I know there are hurdles to jump, pitfalls to avoid and obstacles to overcome, but she will do it, just absolutely do it."

ELEVEN

THE GRAFT ATTACKS
THE HOST

O n Monday, August 10, the medical team arrived early. My gastrointestinal system was high on their agenda for attention that morning. I was still constantly either nauseous, or vomiting, and my digestive system just wasn't functioning. If I wasn't able to start eating soon, they told me, they'd have to do an exploratory procedure to look around in my stomach and see if the problem was due to graft-versus-host disease. They told me they had a strong feeling I had "gut GVH"—meaning that there was a fight breaking out between my body and Chris's marrow, and my stomach was the boxing ring.

I sat up in bed and listened as Dr. Doney ticked off the rest of my problems. My hematocrit had suddenly taken a dip, which meant I was going to need a red blood cell infusion. Due to concern that the cytomegalovirus might be coming at me from within my own body, they were going to put me on a randomized study of another drug, ganciclovir, to see if it could protect me. Of course, it was a double-blind clinical trial, so I wouldn't actually know if I was on the drug or receiving a placebo. If I was on the drug, however, it might suppress my white blood cell counts, and hamper the work of my new marrow, which was exactly what we wanted to avoid.

I tried to take all this in, view all that was happening from a slight distance, be my usual diligent reporter self. What if the study randomized me into the group taking the drug, and it hurt my new marrow? I asked. I would be taken off the drug, the team assured me. But what if I was one of the patients getting a placebo, and it looked like I might get CMV? They would put me on the drug, they promised. I was so exhausted I could barely listen as they explained it all. It was very confusing—just the other day they seemed to be telling me things were going great, now they were telling me there were all these new dangers.

"That's just the way it is with transplants," one of the physician's assistants told me. "You just have to take one day at a time. And things can go backward as well as forward."

My family tried to keep my spirits up. "We keep telling Laura that things are going so well," my mother wrote in her notebook on the afternoon of August 10. "She feels so exhausted that our encouraging words seem to have little impact. We do it because it's important for her to hear every day that her progress is remarkable. . . . She just needs one day without these symptoms."

On August 12, it looked as though I was having that day. I had to go back to eating solid food before I could even think about getting out of the hospital, and I was having some small progress on that front. I congratulated myself in one of my late-night tape recordings. "I had a day, a real, honest-to-goodness decent day—I ate my first food today . . . I slept practically a whole night. . . . You never sleep a whole night here. Got up this morning, and thought, maybe I feel okay, sat up, felt the bile slide up and down in my stomach . . . puked that up, but it was good to get rid of it, because once you get rid of that, at least you can breathe.

"I've got this goal—if I get the food in me, I get out of here, so I made my first big foray into the food department and asked for a dish of applesauce. They brought what would probably be considered a puny dish of applesauce but it looked totally huge to me. But little by little I began to eat it. And just the sensations of taste and eating were so different. . . .

"I've started to read about food again and every now and then I'll start to imagine biting into a really big juicy slice of pizza with a lot of tomato sauce and cheese. But then I can't imagine it . . . the taste buds are just shot. People say try your favorite food—which for me is pasta with tomato sauce—but I don't want to try it, I don't want to ruin my favorite food, ruin that experience for myself. I want to wait until I'm sure my taste buds are back.

"They promised me this won't last forever but apparently it does for a while, where things just don't taste the same anymore. There is always this kind of slimy coating on your tongue and mouth and you have an incredibly heightened sense of smell, so even if there is just a change in an air current you notice it. Things that might not bother you at all are suddenly sickening. Somebody even had a bag of popcorn out in the hall and I'm demanding, 'What is it?' I even notice people smells more and none of them are pleasant."

That night I asked for pears and Jell-O, but I wasn't able to get them down. I also tried little melba toasts, but they tasted and felt like pencil shavings, and I even tasted the plastic from the wrapper. Dean, the cook, specialized in making little Slurpees and slushes that went down easy for transplant patients, so I asked him to try a combination of orange sherbet and seltzer. I got a few sips of that down, but could not finish it.

On August 13, the nutritionist came for a visit. "You have to be eating 500 calories a day, including ten grams of protein, in order to be released from the hospital," she told me. I had to laugh. Five hundred calories was almost nothing compared to what I usually ate, but now it seemed an insurmountable goal. But I tried, ordering soft, comfortable things like baked potatoes with butter. Art and Chris would sit with me, trying to coach me through it. "Come on, just take another bite," Chris would urge, spooning it into my mouth like a baby. But I'd finally turn my face away, unable to stomach another mouthful.

What little capacity I had for swallowing things I had to muster for my medications. The worst was the cyclosporine, the antirejection drug which was at first given intravenously but now I was taking orally. The oral form had the consistency of heavy mineral oil, and tasted even worse. The nurses showed me how to take it by sucking a plastic stopper-full out of the bottle, then shooting it into a glass of chocolate milk. Then you had to stir it quickly, and chug it like a shot of tequila. I was actually one of those strange people who hated chocolate and hated milk, so this medication was doubly unpalatable. But I had to take it, so I forced it down. It actually sent tremors through me as I swallowed it. After that, eating was even less interesting.

But each day, I forced myself to eat a little more. Things *were* getting better; all my blood counts were improving, and I wouldn't need as many platelets anymore, so that meant Art could go home. Having him leave again depressed me a little, and I knew it would be hard for Chris to be the only man around. He and Deborah would take me down to the physical therapy room in the hospital, where I continued my efforts on the weight-lifting machines. My body tone, which I'd always taken pride in, was just about gone, the muscles I'd built up over years of exercise had become weak and flaccid. Sometimes the strain of the exercises just made me more nauseous. The best thing for me was just to walk and walk.

My husband came for a week's visit just after Art left. We usually spoke on the phone daily, but he had not seen me since I lost my hair, and I was worried about his reaction. He was due to arrive midday on August 15, and said he would check into the hotel, then come over. Instead, however, he came right from the airport to the hospital, arriving an hour earlier than I expected. I heard a commotion at the door as my mother and Chris greeted him, and I felt a mad panic; I hadn't had time to cover my bald head with a scarf or turban. I burst into tears when I saw him, but he handled things well. He came right over, sat down on the bed next to me and rubbed my bald head. "It's very cute, dear," he said. Over the next few days, he worked out of his law firm's Seattle office during the day, and sat with me in the evenings.

Though he had helped me immeasurably in the research, right before I left for Seattle, he had told me that we didn't have enough history to go through this kind of thing easily; it wasn't as if we'd been together ten years and had a reservoir of responsibility and duty built up. My own view was that responsibility and duty was part of any decision to marry someone, that "in sickness and in health" was a serious promise.

It has since become very clear to me from talking to other people facing leukemia and other cancers that the strain of coping with someone else's illness is really the true test of the underlying love in a marriage. Many of them, it is true, had been married for years, had children, and already had been through difficult times together. In those relationships there was never any question that the other person would be there through thick and thin. To be sure, the spouse of the patient must undergo a huge trauma of his or her own, but without that hand to hold, many patients say they never would have made it through.

Andre Fedida, the New York gastroenterologist, had been married to wife Sindy for fifteen years when he was diagnosed with leukemia at the age of forty-one. Their first son had been born with serious complications, "and we'd already been through all the stuff that shakes up a marriage," Sindy told me. When Andre became ill, she rallied to his side. "As nurse, doctor, mother, and wife, I knew I had to get my family through this," she added.

Andre, for his part, says, "If it wasn't for Sindy, I never would have made it." He had a difficult time with graft-versus-host disease after transplant, and experienced some psychoses from all the drugs. "I found myself acting like the type of person I would never believe I could be on the medications," he says. "It never shook her, not for a minute." But Andre remembers that some of the relationships of people he met while at the Hutch didn't make it. "You really see who you can count on in a situation like that," he says.

Bill Tafel of Louisville says the strength of his twelve-year marriage helped him and his wife Rebecca to get through the harrowing days when he was frantically searching for a donor and she was pregnant with their third child. "I wasn't treating her like I should," he says. "There was a lot of pressure for her." It was tough being separated after they decided it was best for her to stay home with their three children while his mother cared for him during his transplant in Seattle. "She is damn strong, and she never questioned that I would survive," he says.

But I also learned that not everyone whose relationship stayed strong had a fifteen-year marriage to fall back on. Adam Smith, the thirty-three-year-old owner of an Atlanta auto dealership, and his beautiful blond girlfriend Kristy, twenty-five, had been living a fairly unburdened life together. Both were jet ski racers, and they traveled all over the country to compete. Each viewed marriage as something you did when and if you wanted to have children, and that was way off in the future as far as they were concerned.

But one day, Adam began to get worried about a chronic sinus infection which was not responding to antibiotics. He asked for a blood test; it came back showing an off-the-charts white blood cell count of 245,000 and rapidly advancing CML. With no sibling donor, he and Kristy began a desperate search for an unrelated match while his father helped with the research to determine how to best treat his disease in the meantime.

Kristy helped him in organizing donor drives around Georgia, and Kristy's mother did the same near her home in Kentucky. The situation was getting desperate as Adam began treatment at M. D. Anderson, where doctors put him on interferon to hold the leukemia in check while the search for a marrow donor continued.

But the closest donor he could find was one who matched on four of the six necessary HLA antigens.

Anderson's strategy of taking out some of the T cells from the marrow made sense for that kind of match, and with Kristy's encouragement Adam decided to go for it. On July 4, two months after his diagnosis, Adam proposed, and Kristy accepted. "My feeling on marriage changed completely," she says. "I knew it was now about a true bond, and a true companionship, about working as a team." They rented out their home, he sold his business to his partner, and they moved to Houston, where Kristy spent the next year caring for Adam at the hospital and later at home. They are now back in Atlanta rebuilding their lives.

Was Adam ever worried about whether Kristy would abandon him? "It never crossed my mind that she wouldn't be there," he says. Kristy, for her part, says she would have been there no matter what, but that being married "gives me a great sense of security about everything."

The week before my thirty-eighth birthday, Marilyn and her husband, Noah, came out to Seattle to spend a week's vacation and to help out in any way they could. By now, I was walking on the hospital grounds almost every day, and they would accompany me outside, or perhaps go with me to physical therapy.

In the evenings, my friends and family would take shifts, some going out to dinner while others kept me company. For the first time, my mother was able to go home and relax in the evenings, after weeks of leaving my bedside only to sleep and eat. "This is a good letting go experience for me," she wrote on August 17. "Up till now I felt as if I had to be here fourteen or sixteen hours a day. . . . Another step for all of us toward our real lives."

After determining that my stomach wasn't getting any better, the gastrointestinal specialists decided to take me off solid food again to see if they could figure out what was wrong. Nothing in any of the

tests they ran indicated definitively whether graft-versus-host disease was ravaging my digestive system, but the symptoms clearly
looked as if it were. They decided to do a gastroscopy—a procedure
that involved snaking a thin fiber optic cable with a small camera
down my throat so they could have a look-see in my stomach.

Marilyn, my mother, and I discussed the graft-versus-host disease issue. Our reading of the literature had convinced us of the
theory that it was good to have some GVH—if the graft from my
brother was fighting with my body, it was also fighting any leukemia
cells that might remain. But if I had too much graft-versus-host disease—if the graft fought too hard against my organs—it could dis-
able or even kill me. "This whole GVH issue is like walking the
high wire without a safety net," my mother wrote in her journal.
"You need just enough of it but not too much."

Chris, whom my mom started referring to as "the platelet fac-
tory," was getting pretty depleted from his continuing donation of
blood products to me, and Art was gone to Peru again, so they decided to give me one more infusion from an outside donor, giving
me hydrocortisone and Benadryl intravenously at the same time to
prevent a recurrence of the bad reaction I had the last time I received anonymous platelets. By now, my own platelet count was on
the rise, as was my white blood cell count.

My mucositis had dried up, but so had my own saliva, and almost everything I drank made me throw up. Finally, some Hawai-
ian Punch, of all things, stayed down. The doctors had me
swallowing antacids such as Maalox as much as possible to keep my
stomach coated, which made me even thirstier, and which also
coated my mouth like chalk.

On Thursday, August 20, my birthday, I was scheduled for my
gastroscopy. My mother accompanied me into the room for the
procedure, which began with a strong sedative being pumped into
my bloodstream. That put me out of it enough to allow little awareness of what was happening to me. I do remember a vague sensa-

tion, as if in a dream, of my throat opening up like a canal as someone began to slide what felt like an electrical cord down into my
body. But that was all I remember. My mother, standing next to the
doctor, got to watch the image on the video monitor as the minia-
ture camera traveled into my stomach.

"Amazingly good views . . . some edema and rawness all the
way down from the esophagus into the intestines . . . Dr. feels it's
mild GVH . . . will do biopsy and culture to see if there's an infection . . . Laura KO'd . . . out for the count," she scribbled.

The next thing I remember was waking up in my room, "Happy
Birthday" banners and balloons strung up everywhere, the hospital
staff coming in en masse with my friends and family and a chocolate
cake with blazing candles, singing "Happy Birthday." There were
cards and presents, and general merriment that I struggled to stay
awake for. Everyone else got to enjoy the cake.

Finally everyone left. My stomach still traumatized from the invasive endoscopy, I started to throw up, and did so every hour or so
for the rest of the night. In between, I read over my birthday cards,
including a goofy one from Chris. But inside, under the jokey
punchline, he had written something more serious.

"It's so very hard to put into words how strongly we all feel
through this episode of our lives except to say how very much I love
and care for you. I wish you were not suffering, I wish we were not
here, I wish this did not happen. . . . The one thing I do know for
certain is that you will fully recover and we shall all return to our
normal lives before too long. And here's one other thing I know for
certain: I got off easy, for I would give my life for you."

I tried to stop myself from weeping, reminding myself that it
would just make me throw up more. I felt as if my family *had* given
their lives over to me. I had to get my life back, but I had to give
them theirs back too.

The next day, at about 3 P.M. one of the doctors came in to tell
us that, yes, in fact I had tested positive for graft-versus-host dis-

ease, but it looked like a very mild case. There was also some of it on my skin. The cyclosporine would continue to fight it, but I also needed to take the steroid prednisone, which had some very unpleasant side effects, including sleeplessness, weight gain, and bloating. I wasn't sleeping much anyway, and I couldn't worry about my appearance now.

"Laura seems relatively satisfied that this will be the approach," my mother wrote. "She truly hates the thought of steroids but understands it may be the choice that has to be made." In fact, I tried to laugh about it. As the nurse came in to start my intravenous steroid drip, I puffed out my cheeks like a chipmunk, "Okay, I'm ready!" I cried. "Very funny," Mom scribbled.

Then, tests showed that I was shedding CMV, a dangerous sign that the virus was re-activating itself within me. This was what the doctors referred to as an opportunistic infection—without an immune system, organisms already inside my own body could rise up and kill me. My defenses had been destroyed and it would be months before they were fully recovered.

But there were more drugs to the rescue. They revealed that I had been receiving the actual drug and not the placebo in the test of ganciclovir, and now the drug would be continued in my regimen for a few more weeks to fight the CMV. To that they would add another strong intravenous antiviral agent, and continue its use until there was no further sign of CMV.

Now it was time for another test of my new bone marrow. After the actual engraftment, this would be the first big hurdle, the first sure sign that I might be on my way to a cure. They would be looking for three things: the percentage of marrow in me comprising my brother's cells, how well the marrow was making new cells, and whether there was any sign of the Philadelphia chromosome, the marker for my type of leukemia. As the nurses drew the sample from a needle biopsy in my backside, I tried not to think about what it meant if the results of the test weren't what we wanted.

On August 25, I woke up feeling relatively well—I wasn't nauseous, I managed to swallow a little water, and even ate some applesauce. My father arrived to stay for a week, which lifted my spirits immensely; just seeing his face made me feel good. "She's so much herself that I was shaken by that self's presence—a glimpse of the return of the original," my mother wrote.

At about 10 A.M., Norm Finance, the physician's assistant, came in smiling, "Well, your marrow is making red cells, white cells, and platelets," he said, "and there's no evidence of the disease!" If all went well, he added, "You could be out of here in a few days." My parents were there, as were Chris and Deborah, and everyone broke into a cheer, and soon we were crying, hugging, and laughing. Still I wanted to know more.

"Wait a minute, what about the Philadelphia chromosome?" I demanded. If the chromosome was still there, I was in trouble. Norm replied that that part of the test wasn't back yet. Just at that moment, Dr. Doney, the team leader, came in and said confidently, "It won't be there—you won't have it." I looked at her, incredulous. "How can you know that?" She shrugged, smiling. "I just know."

Nonetheless, I wasn't going to believe it until the test actually came back, and I said so. I had trained myself by now to be optimistic without getting my hopes up too high; for this, I wanted concrete evidence. And two days later, I had it. This time, Dr. Doney came in with the team to announce the final test results: 99 percent of the cells in my marrow were Chris's, twenty out of the twenty cells they had looked at for evidence of the disease were negative, and there was no Philadelphia chromosome. This time, everyone was practically leaping around the room with joy. I didn't know what to feel. My mother, for her part, recorded her own thoughts in her journal: "We are a successful transplant! Now to plan the recovery and the survivorship."

But that night, after everyone left, I again started talking into my tape recorder, my voice hoarse, crying a little, trying to come to terms with everything. Even with the excellent results so far, there still was much more ahead. I began to realize that I would live with this disease and with the scars of this experience for the rest of my life.

"I have such mixed emotions. . . . Does this mean it's really gone forever? And what if it comes back in the next biopsy? You've got to just take the news—you can't just run around and say, 'I'm cured.' But I could be cured—no, I *am* cured—I've got to have the attitude. My parents' attitude is we're past this, we've beat it. Now there's a slow, long road back to being a human being again who can subsist for yourself.

"They might let me out of here Monday, and there's both joy and trepidation in that. There's going to be a whole new routine to get used to, being an outpatient, and not in the protective cocoon of the hospital—all of September, then Mom leaves me, which is like, eeek! Now you have to face everything. You have to be able to start getting on with life and thank God the big picture worked. But now every little thing could go wrong, germs could attack me, my immune system isn't back yet.

"I'm scared. I've got to get that old confidence back . . . I've got to start getting *me* back—my independence and my strength and my fearlessness. Just remember swimming out to that raft in Anguilla. . . . You were scared, you didn't think you had the strength, you kept saying 'I'm sick, I can't do this, it's so far away, it's so deep in the ocean,' but you made yourself do it. Now you've got to make yourself do things, but you have to be cautious, follow the rules, make yourself watch every little thing and learn how to take care of yourself instead of having Mom do everything for you."

Finally, I told myself, "You have to learn that there will be setbacks but that you'll be okay. You've got to believe that this has worked and that it's going to keep working."

For someone who's been through a procedure like a bone marrow transplant, believing it worked may be the hardest thing of all.

Your body has been through so much, your soul is battered, your psyche exhausted from the sheer effort of going through it. As my fellow CML patient Andre Fedida puts it, "It's like you've been sent to hell, and suddenly someone says you can go home now." Even though you had to trust in the science to go through the process in the first place, you are afraid to believe it could work, just like that. You know all the statistics; there is always the danger of relapse, and there's no way to tell if and when it might happen to you.

But in the end, you have to make yourself believe. You have to summon all the strength and faith that enabled you to get through it in the first place, and turn that strength toward getting your life back. You have to look at the good statistics, and believe you will be one of those in that growing percentage of people who survive, disease-free, and live out the rest of their lives.

TWELVE

GOING HOME

O n Monday, August 31, almost two months after I walked into the hospital, it was time to walk out again. The person who left that day was a strange-looking shadow of her former self. I was now as bald as a cue ball, my face was puffy from steroids, my eyes still were bruised and bloodshot, my skin had a yellowish hue. But no matter how bad I looked, I had everything going for me: strong new marrow making healthy new blood cells, and no evidence of the leukemia.

Getting ready to face the world, I pulled one of my wigs over my head (which made me look almost normal if you didn't get too close) and slipped on a yellow paper mask. As Margaret unhooked the last lines from my IV pole and turned off my pumps, my mother and I gave her tearful hugs, thanking her for everything she had done to make our stay there so much easier. We promised to come back and visit before we left Seattle.

I walked around the floor until I found my physician's assistants, Schiffman and Finance, and gave them a couple of high fives. I waved good-bye to some of the other patients on the floor, and walked out into the hall with Deb and my mother. As I stepped into the elevator, the first thing that popped into my head was a favorite phrase from high school: "I'm outta here!"

Chris and my father were in the rented Taurus waiting in front of the hospital. They hustled me into the car for the short ride down to the Marriott Residence Inn. My mother was armed with a bag full of drugs and equipment, including a portable pump that she had learned to operate over the previous few days at a special class. Though I would come back to the outpatient department every day for monitoring, and get most of my serious IV drug infusions there, I still needed to get fluids, nutritional supplements, and some other drugs around the clock, and administering those would be her department.

We settled in for a couple of hours at the Marriott, where I attracted a few curious looks with my mask. At four, we went for our first visit to the outpatient clinic, to meet the staff who would follow me on a daily basis until I was well enough to go back to New York. The amount of information we had to process was mind-boggling; I knew it must be even more confusing for people whose mothers weren't nurses like mine. I got a list of IV and oral medications, which basically divided my entire day into an hourly schedule of drugs, drugs, and more drugs. The staff did a run-through with me and my mother as she hooked up my ganciclovir and got the pump working.

Almost immediately, we had a taste of just how hard the separation from the hospital would be. There someone was always available to help; back at the Marriott, when it was time to add a second IV bag, the instructions just weren't clear, and Mom spent a grim hour trying to figure it out, then hours waiting with trepidation to see if she'd be able to attach the third bag for the night. She called the outpatient clinic a few times to tell them of the problem she was having, and they tried to steer her through it long distance.

The staff was on call twenty-four hours a day to help with outpatient problems, but basically you were on your own. Caregivers of transplant patients frequently say the biggest stress comes after they leave the hospital, when the tasks usually performed by the nursing staff have to be carried out by families. Advances in technology allow patients to be let out of the hospital sooner, and some centers are moving toward doing the entire transplant process on an outpatient basis, with patients and families coming in for treatment every day but living in special housing near the hospital.

Dr. Abrams and her group at the Hutch recently concluded that demands and responsibilities for families have increased "exponentially," especially as hospitals, in an effort to reduce costs, try to minimize the amount of time transplant patients stay in the hospital. Dr. Abrams's studies found that about 80 percent of the caregiving tasks fall to women, and that the medical establishment needs to establish better procedures to help caregivers cope after the patient has returned home.

Indeed, while my mother had moral support from Chris and Deborah for most of the time I was in the hospital, supplemented by visits from my dad and Art, we were to be alone for most of our time in the outpatient phase of the transplant. My father had to get back to work, as did Chris, and Deborah, her Italian sabbatical over too, was returning to her home in California to start her own consulting business. When Chris left the first week of September, I felt completely bereft. It was almost as if I were attached to him by some invisible artery. "I'll be back in a heartbeat if you need me," he told me as we embraced before he left for the airport.

My friend Nancy arrived to be with us during my first few days out of the hospital. At that point we decided it was time for me to start venturing out in the world. We chose a sprawling park not far from the hospital, left the car in an uncrowded section, and wandered along some wooded paths, ending up in a big gazebo. My mom took a picture of the three girls, Deborah and Nancy on either side propping me up, my wig slightly askew as I pulled down my mask and offered a wobbly smile.

But a couple of days later, Nancy had to return to New York, and then Deborah was gone, too. My mother and I waved good-bye as she headed down the long corridor to the elevator at the Marriott, her mane of blond hair swinging out behind her, her energy and presence vaporizing out of our lives for now.

My mother and I settled into a routine. She still changed the dressing on my Hickman catheter every morning, trying to get me to watch her so I could start learning how to do it myself. But I couldn't face it yet, and I still didn't want to touch the tube protruding from my breast.

My mother seemed to have boundless energy. She was sixty-four at the time, and as she bustled around taking care of everything, she reminded me of how she had been back in the days when she was a young working mother who seemed never to be off duty. She had been the Florence Nightingale of the neighborhood, always ministering to some hurt kid. Our house was on the corner of a quiet side street and a busy thoroughfare. More than once I remember my mother running out to the front lawn to tend to an automobile accident victim until an ambulance arrived.

When we were teenagers she worked from 7 A.M. till 3:30 P.M. in the intensive and coronary care units of the local hospital, getting home each day at the same time we arrived from school. She would whiz around like a white tornado cleaning house and making dinner for the family. Often she didn't have time to change out of her uniform. Covered with bloodstains and worse, my mother would regale us with tales of her patients and emergencies. Once in a while we would have to beg her to skip a particularly gruesome tale so we could eat peaceably, but her stories did have the effect of getting us over any squeamishness about medical matters.

Despite the problems and occasional setbacks, my mother had been basically unflappable throughout our stay in Seattle. That portable intravenous pump certainly tried her patience—it never seemed to function correctly, and she had to push the buttons so hard to program the contraption that she would hurt her fingers, and usually had to resort to using the dull end of a spoon or knife.

She was determined not to let it get the better of her, though. She was also the keeper of the schedule, and the administrator and preparer of drugs. From the time I woke up in the morning I had to start swallowing pills, and she would meticulously cross each one off the list as I choked it down.

Because I still couldn't stand to swallow most of the pills, my mother bought a mortar and pestle at a local kitchen shop so we could grind the pills into powder and then mix them with pear, peach, or apricot nectar. I started my mornings at 9 A.M. with a dose of the steroid prednisone, chased down with 300 mg of labetalol (to keep my blood pressure down) and Cardizem (to support my cardiac function and help keep the blood pressure under control). At 10 A.M., it was time for my cocktail of cyclosporine mixed in chocolate milk. By noon, it was time for the estrogen and progestin drugs, Premarin and Provera, which I was taking to restore the hormones I was no longer making now that the chemotherapy had destroyed my ovarian function. Before I ate lunch I had to take Carafate, an ulcer drug which helped neutralize acid in my stomach.

When 3:30 P.M. rolled around, it was time for a 400 mg tablet of fluconazole, an antifungal drug, a couple of doses of the antibacterial pill Bactrim, and a multivitamin. Three or four times a day I had to take Maalox tablets to combat the effects of all this medication on my stomach, and there was always either fluids or ganciclovir running on my portable IV. Most afternoons we headed up to the clinic for blood work to test the levels of cyclosporine in my body and to get an intravenous dose of immunoglobulin, which I needed to help restore my immune system. After dinner, at about 9 P.M., it was time for more prednisone and labetalol, and then a nightcap of cyclosporine in chocolate milk at ten.

I was asked to participate in a study that involved taking cyclosporine for two full years after transplant, instead of the standard six months. The study's aim was to see if the longer course of the drug would protect patients from getting chronic GVH, the kind that could show up as long as a year after transplant and cause all kinds of misery—including death. Avoiding that seemed like a reasonable goal to me.

My mother and I pored over the documents describing the study. According to the data, studies in Japan and Europe showed that prolonged cyclosporine treatment seemed to decrease the risk of chronic GVH. I went to the page on risks: hypertension, transient blindness, convulsions, and other problems, all of which were reversible. Side effects were nausea, fatigue, tremors, headaches, and depression. None of this sounded like anything I didn't already have, and the other side effect was hirsutism, which means that extra hair might grow on me. I didn't have any hair on me at the time, so I figured it couldn't be that bad. I signed on the dotted line.

Meanwhile, the steroids I was taking to control the acute GVH in my stomach had the effect of increasing my appetite. I was eating, but I still wasn't eating enough to get off of the intravenous nutrition. With a fairly light diet of hot cereal in the morning, a sandwich at lunch, and a little chicken for dinner, a week or so after I got out of the hospital, my weight had plunged about ten pounds. "If you don't start eating pretty fast, we may have to put you back in the hospital," the nutritionist warned me after weighing me at the clinic. "Try eating some things with more calories—forget all your good habits and have some fat!"

Convinced, I started in the next morning, frying myself up a couple of eggs and bacon, and making them into a sandwich slathered in Miracle Whip—a breakfast I used to eat as a teenager. I started adding cheese to my sandwiches and ate real ice cream, something I had rarely touched since the invention of low-fat frozen yogurt. I felt emboldened enough to start making trips to a nearby supermarket with my mom, wearing my wig, a cowboy hat pulled down low, and, of course, my mask. Self-conscious, I would pull the mask down around my neck as we walked into the store, then pull it back up if anyone got too close. It had been drummed into me to be extremely careful about contact with other people who had germs to which I had no immunity.

But I was so happy to be out shopping for anything, and to be eating real food again that I didn't much care what fellow shoppers thought about my unusual appearance. I started poring over recipes in women's magazines, and we stocked up on the ingredients they called for. I walked up and down the fruit and vegetable aisles just touching things, quizzed the deli clerk over whether smoked or baked turkey was better, and debated with my mother over the merits of buying prepared chocolate milk versus Hershey's chocolate syrup to put in regular milk for my daily cyclosporine. These were big decisions.

The steroid prednisone had another side effect, making me sleepless and slightly manic. I would sometimes wake up at four in the morning and start typing notes into the computer, sending them by phone modem to various coworkers, driving everyone back in the office a little nuts. I was eager to start reasserting myself at the paper, and was actually grateful when Alix Freedman, who had been editing some stories for my group, called me for help on a page-one story she was trying to whip into shape for one of the reporters. I stayed up all night rewriting it. "I guess I can still do it," I told Alix on the phone. "Just get back here," she pleaded. Heaven knows I wanted to.

I rarely slept more than two or three hours at night. I couldn't lie down prone; if I did, I felt as if I were falling off the earth. I had to have a half-dozen pillows propping me into a half-sitting position in order to get to sleep at all. The mix of drugs I was getting started to send my blood pressure soaring, and none of the hypertension drugs they prescribed seemed to bring it down. As a result, I was feeling lightheaded, dizzy, and disoriented. I would sit in a comfortable chair at the clinic for up to an hour getting my IV immunoglobulin, but as soon as I stood up to leave, I would almost fall over from vertigo. I was trembling, nervous, and irritable.

On Tuesday, September 8, my red blood cell count started to drop, for no apparent reason, and my mother rushed me up to the clinic for two units of donor cells, to be administered along with my immunoglobulin dose. My blood pressure during the transfusion shot up to 190 over 120. The staff then started pumping me with doses of drugs to try and bring it down. After seven hours, with me nearly unconscious in the chair, my blood pressure dropped to a more acceptable level of 160 over 100, and Mom drove me home.

That night, exhausted, I went to sleep early, but woke up at 3:30 A.M. with a pounding headache and heart palpitations. I called out for my mother, who was in the bedroom across the hall. She wanted to take me to the emergency room, but I resisted. In a few minutes the palpitations seemed to taper off a little, and she gave me some Tylenol.

A half hour later, though, at 4 A.M., my heart began to pound so hard I actually could feel my body shake. It completely unnerved me, and I told my mom I wanted to take something to calm my nerves, something that maybe would let me get some sleep. She gave me about 50 mg of Benadryl, a sedative I now used each night, along with Ativan. Finally, I fell into a deep, deep sleep.

At 8 A.M. my mother came to wake me, but couldn't rouse me. I was drenched in sweat, the bed was soaked, and I started mumbling incoherently. Terrified, she tried to pull me up to a sitting position, but my body was like a deadweight. Finally she hoisted me up and took me into the bathroom, where I sat down and urinated, but then couldn't figure out what do with the toilet paper. When I stood up, I walked into a wall. Mom started talking loudly, trying to get me to focus, terrified that I might have had some kind of stroke. In her nurse's voice, she began asking me questions to see if I had any idea where I was.

"Where are you, Laura?"

"In Pittsburgh," I mumbled.

"No, where are you?" she asked again.

"Far from home," I replied.

"Where? Where far from home?" she pressed me.

"In the hospital," I answered this time.

My mother got on the phone to the outpatient clinic; they said they would send a "cabulance"—a van equipped to transport wheelchairs—right away. By the time it arrived, I had started to become a little less disoriented, but I was still pretty much out of it. The driver came up to the room, helped pile me into the wheelchair, and sped me to the clinic. There, the staff quickly determined that I hadn't had any kind of a stroke—my neurological exam was essentially normal and my blood pressure was actually dropping.

They concluded that I must have had some bad reaction to the Benadryl because of my high blood pressure, and because I was also dehydrated. So I lay in one of the outpatient beds while they ran fluids into me for the next several hours, my mother sitting nearby, watching me anxiously. She relaxed a little at 2 P.M. when I sat up and asked for a tuna-fish sandwich. But in her notes that day, she wrote, "Can't even find the usual element of humor in this fearsome day . . ."

I soon learned not to be too discouraged by such setbacks. By the next day, I felt much better—so good, in fact, that I told my mother we were going out for a walk. This was to become our new afternoon routine—we would cross the broad avenue in front of the Marriott and cruise the sprawling marina that stretched along the north shore of Lake Union, or we'd drive over the hill to Lake Washington, the huge recreational lake in the eastern part of the city, and walk along its jogging and bike paths. I finally was getting some energy back, and I also was getting seriously worried about the saggy appearance of my butt.

My blood pressure continued to be a problem, and my magnesium levels were dropping because of the antirejection drug cyclosporine which caused patients to shed magnesium, the mineral that is crucial to building bones, making proteins, conducting nerve impulses to muscles, and helping the body adjust to cold. To correct the deficiency, I had to spend a few hours every other day at the clinic hooked up to a magnesium drip.

Though I still looked puffy around the face from steroids, my weight dropped down to 117, the lowest it had been since I was in junior high school, which set off a round of alarm bells. The clinic told me to keep a log of my food intake, then told me to start eating even more. At least I was finally taking in enough liquid to get off my intravenous fluids, a cause for celebration. On September 25, a test showed I was no longer shedding CMV, which meant I could stop taking the drug ganciclovir.

Finally, on October 1, another marrow biopsy once again showed no trace of the Philadelphia chromosome, no sign of the leukemia, and nothing but Chris's marrow, working away.

By now, summer was over. The hot and sunny days began getting cooler. Seattle's famous clouds began to gather most afternoons. My mother and I bundled up for our walks and our drives around the Puget Sound area. But now I was about to lose her; she had exhausted her three-month leave of absence and was due back at work in Pittsburgh. I had two more weeks to go, and we agreed that I couldn't be completely alone. So my father flew in to spell my mother for the first week, then my husband would come in for a few days after that, and finally my friend Nancy had arranged to be there to escort me on the final voyage home.

I finally was able to stop wearing my mask around others, and began to accept a few visitors; I figured it was time to start facing the world again. One afternoon, my movie producer pal, Dawn Steel, flew up from Los Angeles for a visit to the set of the movie *Sleepless in Seattle,* which seemed ironic, given that the title pretty much described my state, as well. We sat on the sundeck and ate tunafish sandwiches my mother made for us, and I got to tell her that her creative visualization thing hadn't been such a bad idea after all. (Dawn was not far away from a terrible health crisis of her own; to my great sorrow, five years later, she died of a brain tumor.)

The following week, Irving Azoff, an executive who was one of my favorite characters in the entertainment business, asked if he could fly up for lunch with some surprise visitors. Though I had no idea whom he might show up with, when I answered the door I was thrilled to see a couple I was truly fond of, Rob Fried, a producer, and Nancy Travis, an actress. I decided to make my first foray back into the restaurant scene, taking them all across the street to a waterfront seafood place. I was so paranoid at first I could barely eat my grilled tuna, but I managed to digest it without repercussion. "So you're fine," was Rob's estimation.

As my mother prepared to leave in early October, I wondered briefly how I would get by without her. I should be okay—she had taught me how to dress my own bandages, and all the intravenous drugs were being administered at the clinic now. But she had been my most constant companion, my nurse, my best friend. We had bickered and sometimes grown impatient with each other, just like any mother and daughter, and at times I had felt resentful that I was so dependent on her. The day after my father flew in from Pittsburgh, Mom and I embraced, both of us teary as she got ready to leave. She would be so far away from me now, so hard to get to if I needed her. "Everything's going to be all right now, Laura," she assured me. "We beat this thing."

After she left, I took a good look at my father; he appeared to be about ten pounds lighter than the last time I had seen him. Never one to eat big meals—he liked to graze on peanuts, apples, and Hershey's Kisses—he had been subsisting on salads and cheese sandwiches and the occasional fast-food meal while my mother had been with me. I vowed to cook for him now, dragging him with me to my favorite supermarket. Back at the Marriott, he gave me a wide berth as I went to work in the kitchen, unaware of what a mess I was making with my shaky hands and still not-quite-there sense of balance and spatial relationships. Luckily for him, there was a Burger King across the street.

Accompanied by my father, I ventured even farther afield, going to visit a salmon spawning farm and a waterfall thirty miles outside of Seattle. I was feeling well enough by now to enjoy the time alone with him, and luckily for both of us, there were no crises that called for the kind of nursing duties at which my mother excelled. The day he left, my husband arrived to spend a week; that time also proved uneventful, and finally, the outpatient clinic announced I could go home to New York within the next few days.

Since my husband wanted to be in Boston for a law school reunion, Nancy had arranged to swing through Seattle on her way from a business trip to Dallas. I began the preparations for going home, shipping back to New York the awesome amount of stuff I had accumulated. By now I was driving the short distance to the outpatient clinic; it was scary but exhilarating to be mobile again, to be behind the wheel of a car.

I booked a flight for Nancy and me on October 20, but then began to fret about flying back to New York on a commercial airplane. The idea of being on a giant jumbo jet filled with hundreds of people coughing and sneezing scared the bejesus out of me. I asked for advice from one of the staffers at the outpatient clinic, and she told me I would have to be very careful, try to get a seat not too close to other people, and wear my mask for the entire flight. She said people in my situation sometimes took the red-eye back East because it was less crowded. She also mentioned the Corporate Angel Network, a nonprofit group that provided free transportation for cancer patients and bone marrow donors by using empty seats aboard corporate aircraft operating on business flights.

But as luck would have it, my own flight angel appeared. A week or so before I was planning to leave, I called on an old friend who had once volunteered the use of his private plane to take me to Seattle. He again urged me to use it, this time for the return trip. I hesitated, thinking it was too much to ask, but then thought about the daunting task of getting in and out of two crowded international airports like Seattle-Tacoma and JFK with my mask and the insecurity I still felt about being out in the world. When I told him I'd like to take him up on the offer, he said, "Just tell me when you want to be picked up."

Finally, the time came to leave. Though I had promised to go back up to the transplant ward and say good-bye to everyone, I realized I really didn't want to go there again. I wanted to look ahead, to shake the memories of the hospital for now. I called my favorite nurse, Margaret, and my two physician's assistants, and said my final good-byes on the phone. I promised that they would see me again when I returned to Seattle for my one-year checkup.

I met with Dr. Storb one more time in the outpatient clinic, and gave him a big hug. He had been the first person I saw when I came seeking help at Fred Hutchinson, and here I was, almost six months later, saying good-bye. In that time I had been transformed from a frightened, sick woman uncertain of her chances of survival into a new version of myself, with another shot at life.

True, it had been a big, cohesive team of professionals who had helped me get there, a group effort from the lowliest lab technician to the Nobel Prize–winning scientists. And Dr. Storb would be the last one to take credit for my recovery, but to me he would always be a hero, all the more so for his modesty. I hoped he would also always be a friend.

Almost a year to the day after I was diagnosed with leukemia, I had good reason to hope that I had beaten it. I knew the next phase wouldn't be easy, and that I would have to watch myself every step of the way. I wasn't exactly sure what was in store, but I did know that it was time to get back to my own world again, to pick up where I had left off, to resume the business of just living.

Gathering the last of my things, Nancy and I checked out of the Marriott that had been my home away from home. A taxi sped us to the airfield, where our plane was already waiting. We drove right up alongside it and climbed aboard. As the plane began to speed down the runway, I was torn between my feelings of relief at going home at last, and sadness at leaving this beautiful place where I felt I'd been born all over again. When we lifted off, and began our ascent, I pressed my face to the window, straining for one last glimpse of the mountain that had been my beacon of hope during the long months in Seattle. Sure enough, there it was, floating just above a blanket of clouds, the summit of Mount Rainier, sparkling in the sun, white and silvery blue. "Good-bye," I whispered as it faded into the distance behind us.

The future stretched out before me, straight ahead.

STARTING OVER

Returning to your regular world after surviving cancer is much like reentering the earth's atmosphere from space. It takes a period of adjustment before you can resume normal life, and your journey has opened your eyes to things most of the people you encounter can never really understand unless they've been there.

New York was much as I had left it. As I pulled up in a taxi to my apartment building, the doorman didn't recognize me for a minute, then fell all over himself trying to help me. Over the first few weeks, I began reconnecting with my friends a little at a time, taking visitors in short, small doses. I was determined to go back to work by the beginning of January, and I wanted to rebuild my stamina as much as possible.

In late October, it was still mild and sunny most days. Since I lived just a block from Central Park, I started taking long walks, marveling at the brilliant fall foliage. Inside the park the sounds of the surrounding city were muffled to a hum. Soon, I took off my mask, though I still kept my distance from people and avoided crowds. I delighted in putting on my favorite clothes again. Weekdays, I wandered around the cavernous, nearly deserted halls of the Metropolitan Museum of Art, and went to afternoon movies by myself in nearly empty theaters.

I still had my Hickman catheter, and a couple of times a week, a home health care company came to administer intravenous doses of drugs I was still taking to build back my immune system. But over time I was able to cut out most of the other drugs. I had agreed to take the antirejection drug cyclosporine for eighteen months as part of the long-term study, but the drug was giving me tremors, and the hirsutism mentioned as a side effect was getting to me—I had more hair on my face than I did on my head. It was just a soft layer of pale fuzz, but I couldn't stand it.

More important, I was also worried that the immunosuppressive properties of cyclosporine weren't worth the benefits of protecting me from chronic graft-versus-host disease. I feared that the drug might actually be working against my new marrow, a possibility I knew about when I signed on to the study. My GVH symptoms had subsided, and I felt confident that the danger of GVH had subsided as well. I called Storb to discuss all this with him, and he agreed that if I wasn't comfortable with the long-term study, I should stop taking the drug.

Finally it was time to get the tubes removed from my body. I was elated that I would be freed from this apparatus. Out of necessity I had learned to clean and dress it myself, but I hated doing it. I decided to let Sloan-Kettering do the removal job, figuring they certainly had enough experience to perform this simple procedure.

At the hospital, I lay down as instructed on an operating table and almost jumped off again when I saw the doctor was about to pull the tubes out without any kind of anesthetic. "These should come right out—you won't feel more than a gentle tug," he assured me. But the fibers in my body had somehow knit around the rubber tubing, and I was soon entreating him to stop as he yanked harder and harder at the catheter. It literally felt as if he were ripping a tendon out of my body.

"If you don't give me something for this pain, we can't go through with this," I told him between clenched teeth. Finally, he asked someone to get a mild sedative with a painkiller, and in the end, he extracted it with minimum additional pain. The hole in my body soon closed up. What was left was an ugly round scar that fades a little each year.

For a long time it was hard to look at myself in the mirror. My hair was beginning to come back, though at first it was just a soft covering of dark fuzz. My face was fuzzy too, and still a little puffy from steroids. I hadn't worn contact lenses or makeup in months, and it took a couple of days to get used to having the lenses back in my eyes. It took weeks to feel comfortable wearing contacts again for long periods.

The toughest thing was learning to hold my hand steady enough to apply eyeliner and mascara. I had been wearing makeup since I was a teenager, and as a grown-up I don't think I ever appeared in public without it. Over the years I had gotten the application down to about two minutes; now, it took me about ten minutes and several botched attempts before I could walk out of the house without looking like a kid who'd been playing in Mom's cosmetics box.

I faced many restrictions at first. I wasn't able to use a public swimming pool for a year. It also took me a year before I could enjoy a glass of wine with dinner without getting ill. I often got sick for no apparent reason after eating some seemingly normal food. I tired easily for a long time, and it was a long hard road to get back into good physical shape. I am still not where I was before the transplant.

Sometimes coming home after a transplant is almost as traumatic as going through one. For some patients I later got to know, it is even harder. Emory University history professor Judith A. Miller remembers only too well the depression she sank into after her 1993 transplant. "During the transplant I was adrenalized and I took charge, and I felt I could go with the flow," she recalls. Her parents were there to look after her. But she was single and relatively new to Atlanta; when she got out of the hospital and was finally left alone by family and friends in her apartment, she says, she had "a big crash."

She didn't want to rely on anyone, yet she needed help with many things. She didn't feel ready to come back to her full-time teaching load, and struggled with the university over the issue. But then she discovered the BMT-Talk e-mail discussion group, which helped her connect to others with the same problems. After one subscriber posted a question, "Is it normal to feel as mean as a snake after a BMT?" she replied quickly, "Oh yes. Your feelings are very normal. The drugs, stress, and emotional upheaval of a BMT can throw anyone into snakedom."

Later, writing about her experience in the *Blood and Marrow Transplant Newsletter,* she described how hard it was for an independent woman to have to ask for help, and to be so dependent on friends and family. She described "obsessive thoughts and irritability" caused by the drugs she was using, she wrote of depression, and even of hating people who tried to cheer her up. But she described putting her life back together, concluding, "While the snakes are out there during the recovery period, so are miracles, all part and parcel of returning to the life you love."

Miller told me that gradually things began to improve, and she started to enjoy music, to taste food again and to feel like teaching. She began trying to have fun, delving into her research, and tackling some problems she was facing at Emory. Miller remembers that when she was first diagnosed, she was terrified of losing her identity as a historian, and the job she had worked so hard to get. "I love teaching, and it brings me great joy," she says. "The fear of losing all that was even worse than the fear of losing my life." Today, she has tenure at Emory, and she recently completed a book about the history of the grain trade and capitalism in France.

I was relieved to learn that many of the feelings and problems I found myself having after the transplant were shared by others in the same situation. Dr. Abrams and her group at Fred Hutchinson

studied 118 patients three years after their transplants and found a
wide range of common problems. Some were physical: a decrease
in strength and stamina, headaches, skin problems, difficulty sleeping, and pain. But there were emotional problems too. Significant
numbers—often more than half—reported they were easily annoyed, had mood swings, were less tolerant, easily frustrated, and
depressed. This seemed to be equally prevalent among men and
women.

A significant percentage of patients also reported that they had
problems just thinking; they experienced memory problems, difficulty concentrating, and a hard time thinking clearly and express-
ing ideas. This situation can be extremely frustrating. I often found
myself forgetting that I had talked to someone only moments after
our conversation. My mind wandered more frequently. Obviously,
none of these traits were helpful in my profession. For the first couple of years after the transplant, I ran my life with a series of lists
and Post-it notes, until I trained myself with some effort of will to
overcome this problem. It still troubles me from time to time.

Dr. Abrams' group also found another problem: sexual dys-
function. Though both men and women reported similar symptoms, a significantly larger percentage of women than men said they
experienced decreased interest in sex, difficulty with arousal, and
diminished sexual satisfaction. Many report being helped with hormone replacement. But some of the single people I have spoken to
personally say they wonder if they will ever have sex again, and they
despair of finding a partner who will understand what they have
been through and who will have the patience to help them come
back into a loving physical relationship.

If you have undergone treatment at a distant center as I did,
when you return home you have to find someone who can look after you, because you will need close monitoring for at least a year. I
decided to return to Sloan-Kettering because its staff at least knew
the basics of follow-up care for a transplant patient. I called Dr.

Carabasi, who, as he had promised, told me he would be happy to take over my care again, but informed me that he had accepted a job in Alabama and would be leaving soon. He recommended a new doctor there, a young Scotsman named Stephen MacKinnon, who knew I had chosen to have my transplant elsewhere and didn't hold it against me. In fact, he told me right off that refusing a T cell depleted transplant at Sloan-Kettering had been a smart choice for me. "You did absolutely the right thing," he assured me. He has since left the hospital to return to England.

Of course, science and medicine are moving at a rapid pace, and much has changed in the years since I made these decisions. Sloan-Kettering and other transplant centers continued to pursue the use of T cell removal, particularly for patients with acute leukemias, those with unrelated donors, and older patients who might be at greater risk for complications from graft-versus-host disease. As for its patients who have relapsed, Sloan-Kettering says it has been able to get a significant percentage back in remission by administering a dose of their donor's leukocytes.

Dr. Richard O'Reilly, who heads the transplant unit, says today that with advances in their techniques and in treatment of early remissions, Sloan-Kettering's overall disease free survival rate is 70 percent. The success rates are higher, however, in patients with acute myelogenous leukemia, or AML. Dr. O'Reilly stands by all of the work Sloan-Kettering has done in T cell removal, saying the hospital's philosophy is, "You do the best thing you think you can do for the patient." He does acknowledge that in 1991, when I was weighing my options, the issue I was most afraid of—relapse after a T cell depleted transplant—"was a concern." He also acknowledges that for me, going to Seattle "may well have been a correct decision at the time."

What if I were a CML patient, coming to Sloan-Kettering today with a matched sibling donor? For patients under thirty with CML, who have a matched sibling donor, the hospital has abandoned the use of T cell depletion in bone marrow transplants. For patients over thirty, both options—a T cell depleted transplant or a conventional one like I had in Seattle—would be available, and the choice would be up to me. "My read is that you can live with either one," Dr. O'Reilly told me.

For my part, I still strongly believe that I made the right decision, and that for me, the risks of T cell removal outweighed the benefits. I have continued to follow the medical literature on bone marrow transplants, and there have been several scientific studies published over the last few years which conclude that there is a much higher risk of relapse among patients whose donor marrow was first stripped of its T cells. While I am impressed with the progress Sloan-Kettering and others have made in beating relapsed leukemia back into remission by giving the patient donor cells *after* the transplant, I'm glad I didn't have to deal with the issue of relapse at all. And I still would choose Fred Hutchinson over any other center.

But if anything, keeping up with the rapidly changing technology in bone marrow transplantation has made me more certain than ever of the importance of self-education for a cancer patient of any kind. The more you know about the latest science and wisdom in the medical world, the more informed your choices when it comes to the treatment of your disease. Don't assume your internist or even your local specialist is up to date on everything; become a lay expert to the extent possible, and use that knowledge on your own behalf.

Though my doctors in Seattle urged me not to rush back to work, I could hardly wait to return. I put my toe back in the water in December, when, at the request of one of my reporters who was having trouble with one of the companies we covered, I went to that company's chief executive's office to hash things out. I started editing stories from home and checking in with all my old sources.

Right after the new year, six months after I had taken my medical leave, I resumed my daily ritual of heading downtown to the office—this time, however, acting on the advice of the Hutch's Long-Term Follow-Up office, I traveled in a taxi instead of the crowded subway.

As I expected, it was a struggle at first to jump back into the daily hubbub I had been absent from for so long. But difficult or not, I was determined to get things back to normal. I tired easily, but if I got too exhausted I would stretch out on the floor in my office. The great thing about a newspaper is that there is news to worry about every day, and that was the main thing everyone was focused on.

As spring approached, my hair was finally growing back enough to cover my head with a mass of short curls, and I decided I was ready to face the world with my new look. When I walked into the daily 11:00 A.M. editors' meeting without my long-haired wig for the first time, I wasn't recognized for a minute. It was worth it just to see the look on everyone's face before we all burst out laughing. "This is the real me," I told them.

Every six months, I would have to have a bone marrow biopsy, and wait fearfully for the results: would the disease come back, would there be a sign of relapse? But each time the tests came back negative: of the twenty cells examined in a typical bone marrow test, all twenty were male, there was no Philadelphia chromosome, and no evidence of leukemia. My first trip back to Seattle, in July 1993, was a triumph; the one-year mark was considered a big hurdle, and a clean test was a good sign of the future likelihood of disease-free survival. I passed the test with flying colors.

I returned to Seattle once each year, preferring to have the annual checkup there at the hospital that had saved my life. I became well-acquainted with the staff in the long-term follow-up clinic, including Dr. Keith Sullivan and Muriel Siadak, a physician's assistant who was very knowledgeable and experienced with all the aspects of post-transplant issues. My visits were also an opportunity to see Dr. Storb, and to have dinner with him and his wife, Beverly, and catch up on all the most recent advances in treatment at the Hutch and his scull races.

I also liked to visit the transplant ward and say hello to Margaret and all the other staffers who remained there, year after year. It always gave me a shudder at first to get off that elevator on the tenth floor. But it was good to be able to meet some of the patients who were there, and to tell them that not long ago, I had been in their shoes. I think it helped them to see someone who was already back to normal.

For the first couple of years after my transplant, I was so happy to be alive that I didn't much think about whether or not I was truly happy, or about what I really wanted. As most of my friends lamented turning forty, I was thrilled just to get there. But finally, I had to face some painful issues in my own life.

In 1994, I began to explore using my frozen embryos to attempt a pregnancy. It was now two years after my transplant, and I felt more secure that the danger of relapse was diminishing. But there were no extensive clinical studies of post-transplant patients having babies with frozen embryos, and there were a few anecdotal cases indicating that pregnancy itself could pose a threat of relapse.

Dr. McKinnon at Sloan-Kettering gave me two papers describing patients who had successful pregnancies, but had gone on to relapse six months to a year later. He explained to me that the problem might be the natural immunosupression of pregnancy; to put it simply, a woman's immune system naturally suppresses itself so the fetus isn't rejected as a foreign object. But the new immune system created by Chris's marrow was what kept me from relapsing, so suppressing it in any way was potentially dangerous.

I began exploring other options. A colleague put me in touch with friends who used a surrogate mother, and they put me in touch with a center in California that was considered the most reliable surrogate parenting organization in the country. The procedure was expensive, and fraught with legal and psychological dilemmas all around.

And finally, I had to face the truth. While my desire to find some way to have a child with the embryos we had frozen was as strong as ever, my relationship with my husband was not. By 1995, it was clear that the marriage we had made in sickness would not survive in health. I had signed a binding legal document that said I could not use the embryos without his consent, and he had signed the same agreement.

As I considered my options, I came to a painful but necessary conclusion. Having a child was something I wanted, but only if I could do it with someone with whom I would spend the rest of my life, and who would be with me in raising that child. I had no desire to bring a child into the world under any other circumstances. In the summer of 1995, my husband and I separated amicably, agreeing not to use the embryos. They had now been frozen for five years, the limit of time that Cornell had told us they could be confident of the embryos' viability. Though we initially explored donating them to science, Dr. Rosenwaks at Cornell told me the center was unequipped to deal with such a request. We asked that the embryos be destroyed.

In making that decision, I had to face the fact that I would now never have my own biological child, and that was a painful thing to accept. I had to close a door that can never be reopened. Part of me will always wonder what it would be like to feel a baby growing inside me, to know the wonder of its birth, to see my own eyes reflected back at me in those of my child. I will never see the commingled features of my face and the face of the man I love. I will never be able to present my parents with a grandchild so they can see their family continue through me.

People sometimes ask me how I was able to part with the embryos after going through so much to create them. The truth is, having my own biological child at any cost and under any circumstance was never my goal. My original intent had been to preserve the chance of having a baby within the environment of a strong, long-lasting marriage, and to raise that child in a loving family environment like the one I had grown up in. That wasn't going to happen, and there was nothing I could do about it. As for having children, I learned from my friends, like Amy Dunkin and Larry Kraftowitz and their beloved adopted son, Eli, that biology isn't the only way to be a parent; there would be other options open to me if I ever remarried and decided I still wanted to be a mother.

In July of 1995, my parents accompanied me to Seattle for my three-year checkup. The three of us had a wonderful week, journeying to Mount Rainier, visiting all our old haunts, dining with Rainer and Beverly Storb. Most important, I had another clean bill of health and more hope than ever of a healthy future. On the plane back to New York, I finally dared to relax a little, to believe that there was a good chance that I was going to be around for a long while. I had made the decision to end my marriage, and I dared hope that maybe there was a chance for personal happiness in the future. I was frightened and yet elated at the idea of moving on with life. What I didn't expect was just how fast life would move.

The next weekend I attended a party at the East Hampton home of my friend Steve Robert. As I was standing on the patio, drinking a glass of wine, Rick Salomon appeared in the doorway that led to the backyard. The first thing I noticed about him was that he was very handsome, and very sunburned. Something flashed through my mind at that minute, a feeling of all that was possible in life, but I quickly pushed it away. "Don't even think about it," I said to myself.

I hoped that I might meet someone eventually, and maybe find true love, but in truth, I had no idea if it was possible any more, and certainly didn't expect it to happen soon. I was forty-one years old; I had been through a devastating illness; I was lucky to be alive. I had managed to hang on to the things I was afraid I would lose, like my career, and I considered myself blessed to have my family and friends. Perhaps it was too much to expect any more.

In late August, Rick asked me to dinner. By the end of dinner, we both knew something was happening between us. By the end of the week we knew it was serious. Within a month we knew we were in love, and that we would spend the rest of our lives with each other. We moved in together in the fall; six months after we met, on February 16, 1996, we were married.

Though sometimes I wish we had met twenty years ago, I still marvel that we found each other at all. I feel as if the planets some-how aligned, and our lives intersected just at the time when we were ready for each other. It saddens me a little that we can never have a child of our own. But Rick has brought his four wonderful adult children into my life, and I recently became a stepgrand-mother to Wilson Brown Salomon. I look forward to many more, and through my brothers I expect to be a doting aunt one day soon.

Rick knew from the start what he might be getting into by mar-rying me. Early in our relationship, I came down with a bad case of shingles, an acute inflammatory viral disease marked by blistering sores, which frequently plagues transplant patients who are in re-covery. But I was three years out already, and this was another re-minder that my immune system was still struggling to establish itself. The risk of relapse decreases with every passing year; once you make it past the five-year mark, your risk of getting leukemia is considered the same as someone who never had it, but it is there nonetheless.

I told Rick I might never be completely out of the woods. Once you have had cancer, the risk of other cancers is higher. In my con-tinuing research, I read a study published in the *New England Jour-nal of Medicine* in March 1997 which said transplant patients are at significantly higher risk for new solid cancers than is the general population. The risk was 8.3 times as high as expected among those who survived ten or more years after transplantation.

I felt vindicated in my insistence that I not be treated with total-body irradiation prior to my transplant. The study showed that higher doses of total-body irradiation were associated with a higher risk of suffering solid cancers. The fact that I was over the age of thirty when I had my transplant for CML is in my favor as well. Still, risk exists for me. As the study concludes, there is the need for "lifelong surveillance."

Rick and I already have learned how important that surveillance is. In the summer of 1996, he accompanied me to Seattle for my four-year checkup. Again, the standard tests on the twenty cells were negative. But there was an unsettling new development. A more sophisticated test now being used to study post-transplant patients and predict relapse came back with a marginally positive result. Technically, the hospital was calling it "evidence of residual disease."

Instead of looking at twenty cells under a microscope to search for recurrent leukemia, the new test performed a molecular analysis of a sample of 100,000 cells. Using something called a polymerase chain reaction, researchers were now able to find previously undetectable residual malignant cells that might lead to a relapse. What they looked for were so-called bcr/abl positive cells, indicating a fusion of two genes that might be precursors of the disease.

I had paid only slight attention to these tests in the three years after my transplant; initially, the tests had been positive, but my doctors had told me that was considered common after transplant, and they had by the two-year mark become negative. However, I was now a full four years past my transplant. I talked to Dr. Storb by phone in September, and he tried to reassure me, telling me that there had been no more than five or so cells out of the entire 100,000 that registered positive.

"That test might occasionally show the same thing for someone who never had leukemia," he told me. "Your chances of getting leukemia again now are no greater than in the general population, based on our observation of other patients with CML who are this far out after transplant."

But I wasn't taking any chances. In November, Rick and I flew out to Seattle to have the test done again; once again, it came back "marginally" positive. The Hutch was even sending out form letters by then to former patients, saying that a positive test at either six months or twelve months post-transplant indicated a significant risk of relapse compared to those with a negative test.

Dr. Storb and the rest of the team at the Hutch, including Muriel Siadak, our long-term follow-up contact, continued to assure me that they didn't think I had anything to worry about but agreed to monitor my situation carefully with blood tests to look for any alarm bells or changes.

But I decided to do some of my own research once again. In the five years since my diagnosis, the new world of the Internet had changed everything. I had learned to use a Web browser, which helped me discover a treasure trove of direct access to medical papers and studies. Within a day of searching, I found a dozen papers on the bcr/abl tests and their use in predicting relapse. Marilyn Dammerman helped me to analyze them, reprising her role as my expert consultant.

What we found gave me reason both for concern and optimism. To be sure, it was clear that having a bcr/abl positive test was one indicator that a relapse might be coming; a paper from researchers at the University of Michigan and other institutions in the journal *Blood* said that patients with consistently positive tests showed a much greater tendency to relapse, while those with negative tests didn't. They were less sure what to make of patients with mixed tests like mine—some positive, some negative.

"To date, no consistent clinical correlation with clinical out-

come has been identified," the *Blood* paper said. But when we read
all the way to the end, they'd added a note: two more patients with
positive bcr/abl tests had relapsed, making the association of a positive bcr/abl assay a year after transplant with disease relapse "sta-
tistically significant."

"So if this is an early sign of relapse, what do we do?" I asked
Dr. Storb. If it was, he replied, we would do what Sloan-Kettering
was doing with its relapse patients: he would order an infusion of
leukocyte cells from Chris, my marrow donor, or we might consider
interferon. There was some risk to getting another boost of cells
from the donor; as in a transplant, it might trigger graft-versus-host
disease.

But searching through the medical Web sites, I found a report
describing the technique. According to a 1996 study, more than
400 patients who had relapsed after a bone marrow transplant had
been given infusions of cells from their original donors, and as
many as 75 percent had gone back into remission. No more
chemotherapy was needed, nor was further hospitalization required.

I called Chris to talk to him about the possibility that I might
need him again. "You want leukocytes?" was his response. "I got
leukocytes."

By now, I had dropped out of the patient population at Sloan-
Kettering. Dr. McKinnon left the hospital to return to his home in
the U.K., and I didn't want to start over with someone new there if
I didn't have to. A longtime friend, Dr. Eric Neibart, was an infectious disease specialist with a general practice in New York, and he
agreed to do the blood tests I needed and ship them to Seattle for
analysis. Dr. Storb suggested we wait until my official five-year
checkup, which was now only a few months away, to do another
bone marrow biopsy.

I told my family about the new tests, conveying to them Dr.
Storb's confidence that I wasn't on my way to a relapse five years af-

ter transplant. Everyone wanted to believe that, but they also wanted to know for sure. We had always said that we would have a family reunion in Seattle when the five-year hurdle came around, and now we started making plans.

We booked several rooms in the Marriott Residence Inn, our former home. Coordinating everyone's participation was like laying battle plans—Rick and I came from New York; my parents flew in from Pittsburgh; Art, whose company had transferred him to Hong Kong, arranged his business plans around a trip through Seattle; Deborah, ensconced in a new job as vice president of corporate communications at Universal Studios, headed north from Los Angeles; and Chris, now living and working in Atlanta, arrived with his future wife, Penny Cox.

Our first event was a Sunday pilgrimage to Mount Rainier; we rented a minivan and everyone piled in for the two-and-a-half-hour trip. When we arrived, we found the entire mountain, right down to the parking lot, still covered in snow from a rough winter. Wearing nothing but shorts and sneakers—it was July, after all—we left my parents to relax at the ranger station and the rest of us started climbing, higher than we had ever been before, until we were nearly to the point where serious mountain climbers with pickaxes and camping equipment were the only ones passing us by.

Elated, we posed for a picture with the summit of Mount Rainier behind us, then slid practically all the way down the mountain laughing and pelting each other with snowballs. By the time we reached the parking lot again, we were soaked through, and once inside the minivan we peeled off our shoes and socks. On the long ride home we became ravenous, so we stopped at several fast-food and convenience stores in search of junk food, particularly some Ben & Jerry's Cherry Garcia frozen pops that Rick had discovered and become obsessed with. By the time we got back to Seattle, we were weak from silliness. "I think we're all suffering from minivan confinement syndrome," my dad opined. But we had been to the

mountain; symbolically at least, that seemed to me the most important thing before a bone marrow test.

Everyone sobered up pretty fast by 9 A.M. Monday morning,
when we all descended on the outpatient clinic at Fred Hutchinson. While half my entourage paced in the waiting room, I went
back into one of the examining rooms with two of the nurses, my
mother, Rick, and Deborah for the big test. As usual, I asked for
some of those nice drugs to take the edge off. It was almost old hat
to me now, that needle plunging into my hip—and these nurses
were pros who barely let me feel a twinge. As the needle sucked the
marrow out, I clutched Rick's hand, and gazed into his beautiful
brown eyes, still in awe that we had found each other, and praying
there would be nothing to come out of this test that would interfere
with our happiness.

The results of the marrow probe wouldn't be ready until Thursday. Meanwhile, there were a battery of other examinations to en-
dure—tests to see how my lungs, eyes, mouth, and other organs
were doing five years after transplant. The family took side trips to
our favorite Seattle sites and restaurants. By midweek, Rick and I
sent everyone home, promising to call as soon as we received results. On Thursday, we waited alone in the outpatient clinic, where
we had an 11 A.M. appointment to hear the preliminary results from
Muriel Siadak and others on the follow-up team.

But at 10:45 A.M., Dr. Storb appeared in front of us, waving a
piece of paper. "I thought I would give you the scoop ahead of
time," he said with a mischievous grin. He told us the cytogenetic
tests had come back clear as could be—all twenty cells were my
brother's marrow, still fighting the good fight. The more sophisticated tests would be back in just a few days, though he assured me
again, "I think there's going to be nothing to worry about." We
rushed to catch our plane back to New York, telling each other he
had to be right.

Sure enough, a few days later, as I was sitting at the same desk in the same office where I first learned I had leukemia in October 1991, I got another call. This time, it was Dr. Storb with the bcr/abl results: the tests that had been positive before were now completely negative. "I think maybe we got whatever cells were lurking around in there out by taking the tests in the first place." Dr. Storb laughed. And then he said, "Laura, I think it's time for you to relax about this now."

I promised him I would try, but the fact is, I probably never will truly relax. I can only be grateful I've had a second chance at life, and I'll remain vigilant about protecting it. The fear that the disease will come back is never completely gone, but it can be kept at bay. It is hard work getting comfortable with the idea that the bad times are really over, that it's okay to feel happy, loved, and secure. As for my good health, I've learned to enjoy it. But I'm not getting too cocky about anything. Let's just say, so far, so good.

A SURVIVAL GUIDE

Close to 30,000 people are diagnosed with leukemia each year; almost twice that many may hear they have lymphoma, and tens of thousands more will be diagnosed with other blood cancers. A generation ago, these diagnoses were almost certainly a death sentence; today, thanks to rapid advances in hematological oncology, there is a strong chance you can survive the disease and go on to live a normal life.

According to the American Cancer Society, survival rates for all forms of leukemia have tripled over the past thirty years, and those rates are only going to improve. Since 1991 alone, the science of bone marrow transplantation has taken an exponential leap forward. Genetic engineering and gene therapy ultimately will allow doctors to cure leukemia patients with far less radical therapies and toxic regimens than are used today. There are new techniques to alter a patient's stem cells to fight leukemia, attacking the cancerous cells while leaving the healthy ones intact.

Using so-called peripheral blood stem cells, doctors have already found ways to get the crucial cells they need for a transplant from circulating blood instead of having to probe the bone marrow. Sometimes the disease is in the bone marrow but the blood is still uncontaminated; the stem cells in that blood can be used to grow new disease-free blood cells. Even if the blood has already been contaminated, the stem cells can be extracted from the blood, treated with drugs to kill cancer cells, and then frozen until the patient is ready for a transplant.

Doctors are even experimenting with umbilical cord blood transplants, a procedure first discovered by French doctors treating a child who faced death without a bone marrow transplant. The patient's infant sister was a perfect match but too young to donate marrow. So doctors took blood preserved from the newborn's umbilical cord and placenta and transferred those cells into the patient. Scientists are investigating how cord blood could be used to extend transplants to many more people.

As in any cancer, early detection is crucial to increasing your odds of survival. The best advice I can give to someone who has symptoms such as chronic fatigue, a respiratory infection that won't go away, or pain in the spleen area, is to get a simple blood test. Don't procrastinate, and don't let a doctor tell you don't need one. A CBC, or complete blood count, is a standard test that any physician can justify when a patient shows up with the kind of symptoms mentioned above. Time is of the essence once your blood starts going haywire; the longer it takes to find out what's wrong with you, the less chance there is that you can stop it in time.

In the event that you do have leukemia or some other blood cancer, the first thing you need to do is find the best cancer center for treatment. In most large cities you may have more than one choice, while in smaller cities and rural areas you may have to travel fairly far from home. Your health care plan or HMO may require you to use one of its approved providers. Be prepared to do battle if the approved provider is one that doesn't have the best record of treating your particular disease, or doesn't have the best survival rates.

Even if your plan won't pay for another consultation, it is fairly easy to research what is going on at other hospitals. The best way to do this is through online computer services. Most of the key cancer centers have their own Web sites, providing detailed information about the work they are doing. Though many doctors are reluctant to get into an e-mail dialogue, it is often possible to call physicians directly. Some centers, such as Fred Hutchinson, have a rotating oncologist of the month to answer questions. A reference book, *The Best Doctors in America,* can help you locate the specialist you need, and its creators now offer a service, for a fee, that will help you with your specific search for a doctor in your area. The service was featured on CBS's *60 Minutes* as a great resource for patients.

You can accomplish a lot in a phone consult as long as you have boned up on your disease and your treatment options so you can ask intelligent questions. If you aren't computer literate, learn to be, or find a friend who is. It's much easier than you think, and most six-year-olds can show you how to surf the Net. If you don't have access to a computer, visit a friend who does or use one at the public library. There's no excuse not to take advantage of what it offers. There is so much information about cancer now available on the Web that it can be downright mind-boggling. And as with anything, you have to be on the lookout for commercial sites that are trying to sell you something, and even the occasional snake-oil salesman. But if you stick to the reputable Web sites that are clearly connected with government- and university-funded research, or hospitals and legitimate medical journals, it will be well worth your time.

Sometimes just one Web site, such as the Leukemia Links Web page put together by Art Flatau and Barbara Lackritz, will direct you to all the other helpful sites you need, all accessed with the click of the mouse. Sue Stewart's *BMT Newsletter* online includes a resource directory with direct links to both medical sites and financial aid information. You can download her guide to the nuts and bolts of bone marrow transplants free of charge. Also free and easily navigable is data from the National Cancer Institute, the

Leukemia Society of America, The National Bone Marrow Donor Program, and dozens of other resources.

One of the most revolutionary aspects of the Web is its ability to link you up with other people who have been through what you are dealing with and who want to help. Laurel Simmons' BMT-Talk is perhaps the best example of a virtual community of people who reach out each day through cyberspace to help patients and their families deal with the trauma of leukemia and other blood cancers and bone marrow transplants.

Like me, Simmons says that she was able to rely on smart friends to help her in her research back in 1987 when she was first diagnosed with leukemia. But as she told me in one of our e-mail correspondences, "Part of the reason I think it's important to get high-quality support and information on the Net is because not all of us are lucky enough to have a group of empowered and dedicated friends to help us make critical medical decisions, whereas most people in the United States will have access to the Internet in the next ten years."

Don't be afraid to delve into the more scientific resources available to you. If you want to know what the latest research is on your specific disease, at the particular stage it is in, you can immediately access medical journals and even reports of meetings to get the latest information. Yes, the papers are usually in medical jargon, but you can almost always get enough of a sense of what they say—and their conclusions—to determine if this is something about which you should be asking your doctors.

For example, when the American Society of Hematology held its 1997 annual meeting in San Diego, abstracts of all the papers presented there were posted on the Internet. You can search the Web site by disease type; for example, a search of papers on my disease, chronic myelogenous leukemia, yielded a paper on how the use of donor leukocyte infusions for patients who had relapsed after transplant was working for people who had either T cell depleted transplants or conventional transplants like the one I chose. There was a raft of abstracts on the latest developments in peripheral stem cell transplants, developments your own hematologist may just be learning about.

Assuming you have determined you need a transplant but have no sibling donor, your doctor or cancer center will begin the process of putting you through the national and international registry searches. Your center must be accredited with the National Bone Marrow Program to request donors for further testing. The National Marrow Donor Program has all the information you need to know online or will send it to you through regular mail; it also has a toll-free number.

Experts at the Hutchinson Cancer Center say that a few years ago, they expected to find unrelated donors for no more than 20 percent to 25 percent of their patients. Today, for Caucasians under age thirty-five, they expect to find donors for as many as 80 percent; for those aged thirty-five to fifty-five they can find donors for 45 percent to 55 percent. Part of the reason for the increase is improved techniques for identifying those HLA genetic markers and a loosening of the criteria on what qualifies as a match allowing for a less perfect match in younger patients who can more easily withstand complications. Equally important, the national registry has dramatically increased its pool of donors, and with new international registries, the number of potential donors has grown to nearly 4 million worldwide.

Finding donors is still harder for African Americans, Asians, and American Indians. Minorities are still sadly underrepresented in the donor registries. And a transplant from an unrelated matched donor is riskier. The chances of rejection, complications, and infection are higher, the need for extra precautions during transplant crucial. The likelihood of graft-versus-host disease is also greater with an unrelated donor, because the unrelated donor's marrow graft is more likely to recognize the transplant patient's tissues or host, as a foreign body, and start attacking its organs.

A preliminary search is free, and search results are usually available within twenty-four hours. The search identifies people who *might* be a match, but narrowing it down to one who actually *is* a match can get very expensive, with total costs running from $18,000 to $25,000 or more, depending on how long it takes and how many potential donors have to be tested. Some insurance plans will pay for such a search, though many will pay only a limited amount or will resist payment altogether.

The NMDP has an office of patient advocacy that is aggressive in helping to educate insurance companies about unrelated marrow transplantation and you can contact them for assistance in re-filing claims and appealing refused claims. You should keep the pressure on, and enlist your doctors and the Human Resources staff at your employer. The *BMT Newsletter* has useful information about insurance issues as well.

The Marrow Foundation, started in 1991 by the Navy's Admiral E. R. Zumwalt, Jr., to help support the National Marrow Donor Program, also helps patients with financial need in the search process, and has special programs for minorities in financial need. Many patients without insurance or the financial resources to conduct a search have had success with fund-raising drives through local churches and charitable groups.

Once you find yourself in a position to get a bone marrow transplant or stem cell transplant, if fertility is an issue for you, explore your options. Younger people in their teens and twenties can sometimes spontaneously recover fertility after chemo and radiation, but there is no guarantee of that. And the older you are, the less likely it is that that will happen. For men, the decision is fairly easy: you can merely freeze sperm before undergoing chemotherapy and radiation.

For women, the choices are tougher, but getting better. In 1997, researchers finally found a way to freeze a woman's eggs so she can decide later who will fertilize them. The technique is still new, but worth talking to a fertility specialist about. Married couples can go through the in vitro fertilization process now, and store embryos. Again, the chances of success with frozen embryos are still in the 30 percent range at most centers. Along with your cancer specialist, you will have to decide whether your body has the strength and your disease is at a stage where you can take time off from cancer treatment or put off a transplant in order to take the hormone doses you will need to produce enough eggs to complete the in vitro fertilization process.

When it's time for your chemotherapy, radiation, and transplant, hope for the best, be prepared for the worst, and try to take the attitude that you can handle whatever comes at you. A bone marrow transplant is possibly the most radical therapy a human body can sustain. There is virtually nothing in your life that will prepare you for the kind of sickness you will experience, and there's no pussyfooting around that.

I have talked to some people who say they sailed through it, but I can count them on one hand. Everybody comes up with his or her own strategies for dealing with it; sometimes you have to will yourself to shut down your sensory perceptions, almost as if you were going into hibernation or a long sleep. Expect nothing from yourself other than to get through each day, and tell yourself that each day you get through brings you closer to being better again.

But as difficult as a transplant remains, it is getting easier all the time. There are more and better drugs all the time to help you get through it. Pain management is an integral part of transplant units, and the good centers care about minimizing the trauma. Therapy for graft-versus-host disease is improving rapidly. Most important, researchers are finding ways to substantially reduce the toxicity of transplants by cutting back on radiation and chemotherapy doses, and reducing the amount of time a patient has to spend in the hospital. More centers are attempting transplants on an outpatient basis; someday the main treatment may be given in a doctor's office!

Don't hesitate to reach out to the people who love you, for they will be your lifeline. But understand that this is difficult for them too, and that every relationship is likely to undergo some strain. The hardest thing for many patients is the loss of control; if your parent is your primary caregiver, as an adult you will feel like you are a small child again, and you may even resent that. If your spouse is the one taking care of you, recognize that whatever roles you played for each other before will be somehow changed, and many patients have reported that their marriages were strained almost to the breaking point in the process. But for many people, successfully negotiating their way through a transplant brings them closer than ever.

If you have children, the impact can be even greater. Trying to tell kids that a parent is about to go through something as radical as a bone marrow transplant is hard enough; having the children see a parent in that state can be devastating. There are some books out there to help; one is *Mira's Month,* a book by breast cancer survivor Deborah Weinsten-Stern published by the *Blood and Marrow Transplant Newsletter* and available online through the University of Pennsylvania's Onco-Link Web site.

When you finally arrive back home from a transplant, the hardest thing is resuming normal life. Some people who avoid the worst effects of graft-versus-host disease may be able to get back to normal relatively quickly. Bill Tafel was playing tennis a few weeks after his return. But you may still be on drugs like prednisone, which can leave you irritable and edgy, and you may not look anything like your old self for a while. Your face may be puffy from the steroids, and your hair may take longer than you'd like to grow back. It may look different when it does come back, at least for a while.

Your energy level may be high one day and absent the next. You can have a great few weeks and then sink back into exhaustion. Food may not taste the same, and your senses may seem dulled. You may not be able to have sex for a while, and it may take quite a bit of time to get the hang of it again. You will probably have to go on hormone replacement drugs.

Married or not, face the fact that some of your relationships won't make it. If they don't, maybe that is for the best. There is nothing like a crisis to bring out the true colors in people. Some may be good in a crisis but unable to handle the long road back when the crisis is over and the recovery begins. After the trauma of cancer, the idea of losing a marriage may seem unbearable. But remember that almost anything is better than being with someone who can't be there for you.

It would be nice to think that once you've survived, your brush with cancer is over. But in fact, your risks of developing another cancer may be higher than the average person. You must be attentive about follow-up care, and keep up with the latest research. After a while, you won't think about it every day, and the day will come when you can get through a long time without thinking about it at all. But you can never forget it. To borrow from the famous saying about freedom, the price of health is eternal vigilance.

RESOURCES

What follows is a selective list of some of the most useful resources for people facing cancer, particularly leukemia, and related diseases requiring a bone marrow transplant. Most of them are accessible on the Internet. Occasionally a Web site's address will change, but if you type the address into your Web browser and it isn't there anymore, there will usually be a new address posted. The best Web sites contain links to many other destinations that you will find useful. If you really want to browse around, you can simply type the name of your disease, such as "chronic myelogenous leukemia" into an Internet search engine and find a vast array of useful—and not so useful—information. Don't be surprised if some strange things appear on a broad search; some unsavory types have cleverly learned to link their Web sites to search words that include everything from diseases to politicians. I was once helping a friend search for information on a condition called fibromyalgia and one of the results that came up was a porno site.

There are a number of commercial sites which can be useful too, but most of them bombard you with advertising while you are trying to search for serious information. One or two of them are worth the distraction. Generally, the best information comes from nonprofit institutions or from reputable cancer treatment centers and research universities. In addition to their online addresses, many provide toll-free numbers, or can be reached via fax, e-mail, or regular mail.

GrannyBarb and Art's Leukemia Links

http://www.acor.org.diseases/hematology/Leukemia/leukemia.
html

This Web site, developed by the merger of two lists put together by leukemia survivors Art Flatau and Barbara Lackritz, is among the most comprehensive Web sites; once you sign on to it, it provides direct links to many of the best resources, from cancer centers and clinical trials to helpful organizations and leukemia survivors' stories, including their own. It has direct links to medical centers such as M. D. Anderson and Johns Hopkins; and links to medical journals such as *Blood* and *CONIFER,* a comprehensive service providing information on medical meetings and abstracts from recent research papers on hematology.

Blood & Marrow Transplant Newsletter

http://www.bmtnews.org
1985 Spruce Avenue
Highland Park, IL 60035
E-mail: help@bmtnews.org
(847) 831-1913
Fax: (847) 831-1943

Founded by leukemia survivor Susan Stewart, this is a highly useful not-for-profit organization that provides publications and support services to bone marrow, peripheral blood stem cell, and cord blood transplant patients and survivors. The newsletter articles are written in lay language, and reviewed for accuracy by a team of medical experts from transplant centers in the United States and

able, with lots of useful information on leuk
for both patients and health care professic
tion on insurance, clinical trials, and financ

Leukemia Society of America
http://www.leukemia.org
600 Third Avenue New York, NY 10016
(212) 573-8484
Information Resource Center: (800) 955-4LSA

A national organization dedicated to curing leukemia and related diseases and improving the quality of life for patients and families. The Web site also has links to many other helpful scientific sites, patient aid services, and research.

Medicine Online
http://www.meds.com

A free health information service funded by drug companies like Glaxo Wellcome. That means you have to look at drug ads while you are searching, but it links you to the federal NCI data, and allows you to search the abstracts of up-to-date medical papers on your disease via Medline. It also has cancer forums and a useful glossary and links to the online Amazon bookstore to order books about cancer topics.

MEDSITE
http://www.medsite.com
Medsite Publishing LLC
60 East 13th Street, 5th Floor
New York, NY 10003
(212) 253-6913
Fax: (212) 253-9507

commercial site that, once you get past the ads, has very
links to dozens of other sites on a wide range of cancer issues
uding leukemia and bone marrow transplants. It lets you order
books, search MEDLINE, and rates other sites for their usefulness
for patients, medical professionals, and students.

Childhood Leukemia Center

http://www.patientcenters.com/leukemia
O'Reilly & Associates, Inc.
90 Sherman Street
Cambridge, MA 02140
(617) 354-5800
(800) 775-7731
E-mail:nuts@oreilly.com

An online and publishing resource for parents and others caring for a
child with leukemia or other cancer. This center contains material
adapted from the book *Childhood Leukemia: A Guide for Families,
Friends, and Caregivers* by Nancy Keene, published by O'Reilly &
Associates, which also oversees this Web site. The site links you to other
helpful organizations and groups including online support groups, financial assistance resources, and bone marrow donor location groups.

The Best Doctors in America

http://www.bestdoctors.com
E-Mail: info@bestdoctors.com
(888) DOCTORS
Fax: (803) 648-7240

The services of this group are not free; its resource directories, grouped
by region, cost $95 each, and it charges a fee for a personalized search
of doctors specializing in a particular condition such as leukemia.
However, the books are usually available in the public library.

Canada. On the Web site you can search the archives of the quarterly newsletter. You can also read Stewart's 157-page handbook online on the basics of bone marrow transplants and the physical and emotional issues, and *Mira's Month,* an illustrated book for kids whose parents are about to be hospitalized for a transplant. Both can also be ordered via mail.

Stewart's organization also provides patient-to-survivor links, attorney referral services for patients having a hard time with insurance reimbursement for transplants, and a resource directory of other organizations that provide financial support, psychological help or more information. She also has a resource directory with a long list of groups in different parts of the country who help with fund-raising and financial assistance for transplant patients.

BMT-Talk
http://www.ai.mit.edu/people/laurel/bmt-talk.info
E-mail: bmt-talk@mit.edu

Founded by leukemia survivor Laurel Simmons, BMT-Talk is a moderated mailing list for the discussion of bone marrow transplants, and one of the best ways to find other patients who are going through transplants or have already survived them. Once you sign on to the Web address above, it will give you instructions on the simple steps to subscribe. Once subscribed, you will get every e-mail that goes to the mailing list; the best bet is to follow the instructions for subscribing to a daily digest, which means you get one e-mail a day with all the messages tacked on as attachments and categorized by subject matter. You can simply read the mail or send your own mail out to the list; it will be seen by everyone and you may get a flood of responses. Many people on the list will offer to get in touch with you privately as well via e-mail or phone if you don't want your situation broadcast to everyone or if you want to get into a more detailed conversation. You can also search the archives of the mailing list.

Hem-Onc

http://www.acor.org.diseases.hematology/leukemia/hemonc.html

E-mail: hem-onc-request@listserv.acor.org

This is an unmoderated discussion group, related to BMT-Talk, for patients, family, friends, researchers, and physicians to discuss clinical and nonclinical issues and advances relating to leukemia, lymphoma, and multiple myeloma. Run by volunteers, it aims to be a forum for patients and families to exchange experiences on coping with the disease and find information. Like BMT-Talk, once you sign on it will give you instructions on how to subscribe and post questions. It even has photos of the people who have been involved in it, including Art Flatau and Barb Lackritz (aka GrannyBarb), Laurel Simmons, and Emory University history professor Judith A. Miller.

Acor, Association of Cancer Online Resources

http://www.medinfo.org

Acor and its Medinfo service provide direct links to the archives of moderated and unmoderated cancer support groups like BMT-Talk and Hem-Onc. Acor also provides links to CancerNet, which includes the up-to-date research and treatment summaries on various forms of cancer from the National Cancer Institute known as PDQ summaries.

CancerNet

http://cancernet.nci.nih.gov

CancerNet can be reached online directly. The NCI is a component of the Department of Health and Human Services' National Institutes of Health. The NCI is the federal government's principal entity for cancer research and training.

The NIH conducts clinical trials on various diseases and may be conducting a trial that may be of interest to you as a patient. You can search for the kind of trials being done on your specific disease online using a search form provided by NCI (http://cancernet.nci. nih.gov/prot/protsrch.shtml).

The National Library of Medicine

http://www.nim.nih.gov/
(888) 346-3656
(301) 594-5983
8600 Rockville Pike
Bethesda, MD 20894
PubMed: MEDLINE Retrieval on the World Wide Web
http://www.ncbi.nlm.nih.gov/PubMed/

PubMed is a Web retrieval service developed by the National Library of Medicine which provides free access to MEDLINE, a huge database of journal articles that can be searched according to specific diseases such as leukemia. The sites provide help in navigating through the various features. The InterNet Grateful Med Service helps you search for what you need, and the Loansome Doc feature allows you to order studies and research documents free of charge. It will also link you to the National Institutes of Health.

The National Marrow Donor Program

http://www/marrow.org/
3433 Broadway Street NE, Suite 400
Minneapolis, MN 55413
(800) 654-1247

The Marrow Foundation
http://www.marrow.org/tmf/found.htm
400 Seventh Street NW, Suite 206
Washington, DC 20004
(202) 638-6601
Fax: (202) 638-0641
E-mail: tmf@nmdp.org

These are the groups you will need if you have to find an unrelated donor. The NMDP maintains a computerized registry of volunteer donors and will work with your treatment center on setting up a search. Its partner, The Marrow Foundation, helps to secure funding for programs that expand the pool of donors, promotes the diversity of the registry, and provides financial assistance to needy patients in the search process.

Fred Hutchinson Cancer Research Center
http://www.fhcrc.org
1100 Fairview Avenue N.
P.O. Box 19024
Seattle, WA 98109–1024
(206) 667-5000   *(800)-804-8824*
(206) 667-7005   *(206) 667-5001 Intake Unit*

The nation's top center for bone marrow transplants, leukemia, and related blood cancer research. Its Web site will guide you through its medical practice, show you articles about its studies, update you on its research, and allow you to e-mail doctors and researchers directly.

OncoLink
University of Pennsylvania Cancer Center
http://oncolink.upenn.edu/

One of the best on-line resources run by a university medical center, and one of the first oncology sites on the Web. Easily search-